Sonnets to Orpheus

with

Letters to a Young Poet

Also from Carcanet

RILKE
Duino Elegies
translated by Stephen Cohn
illustrations by Elisabeth Frink
preface by Peter Porter

RILKE
Neue Gedichte
New Poems
translated by Stephen Cohn
introduction by John Bayley

Contents

Acknowledgements

I wish once more to thank Peter Porter and Ray Ockenden who generously gave their time and their talent in working on the *Sonnets*.

David Luke was kind enough to read a draft of the *Letters to a Young Poet*, and his notes on my text were of great help to me: my thanks to him also.

SONNETS TO ORPHEUS

Introduction

Beau ciel, vrai ciel, regarde-moi qui change!
Après tant d'orgueil, après tant d'étrange
Oisiveté, mais pleine de pouvoir,
Je m'abandonne à ce brillant espace,
Sur les maisons des morts mon ombre passe
Qui m'apprivoise à son frêle mouvoir.
– Paul Valéry, 'Le Cimetière marin'

'I find an infinite grace in the fact', wrote Rilke to his Polish translator Witold Hulewicz, 'that I was permitted to fill both these sails with the same breath: the small rust-coloured sail of the *Sonnets* as well as the huge white canvas of the *Elegies*.'

The year 1922 saw the publication of Eliot's *The Waste Land*, James Joyce's *Ulysses* (500 copies were incinerated by the US Post Office), Paul Valéry's *Charmes* and Edith Sitwell's *Façade*. It was also Rilke's own great year, in which the *Duino Elegies* and the *Sonnets to Orpheus* were both completed. They were published in the following year.

He had begun his work on the *Elegies* in 1912, at Castle Duino on the Adriatic. Over the years Rilke came more and more to regard them as his life's-project, his *Auftrag* or 'commission'. Between 1912 and 1915 and at various locations he worked on poems in the projected cycle; at Duino itself, at Ronda in the south of Spain, in Paris, and lastly in Munich during the First World War. From this time on his work on the *Elegies* virtually came to a halt and even Rilke sometimes doubted if he would succeed in completing them. The July of 1921, an exceptionally scorching summer, saw the poet for the first time installed in the primitive Château de Muzot, near Sierre in the Swiss Valais. It was the year in which Rilke had come face to face with the verse of Paul Valéry and had made a translation of 'Le Cimetière marin'. His encounter with the French Symbolist signalled a new beginning: 'one day I read Valéry and I knew that my waiting was over'.

Leased for him through the kindness of a benefactor, Werner Reinhart, the little Château de Muzot was perhaps the closest that the poet had ever come to having a home of his own. Dating from the thirteenth century, it is in feeling and scale more a tall manor-farmhouse than what anyone might expect of a 'château' – a 'tower' of great character, dark in tone and with a stepped gable. Here at Muzot during an explosion of inspired and frenzied creative activity, Rilke succeeded in completing the great structure of the *Duino Elegies*.

He was also, to his own surprise, 'given' the two parts of the *Sonnets to Orpheus*. 'They are', wrote Rilke later, 'perhaps most mysterious, even to me, in the manner in which they arrived and imposed themselves on me – the most puzzling dictation I have ever received and taken down. The whole of the first part was transcribed by me in one single breathless act of obedience... with not one single word in doubt or needing to be changed.'

The Sonnets of Part 1 were written between 2 and 5 February 1922: twenty-five poems, one of which was later replaced by 1: XXI, the little *Kinderfrühlingslied*. A twenty-sixth poem, the present 1: XXIII, was later added to Part 1. Between 15 and 23 February Rilke completed the twenty-nine poems of Part 2. The same month of February saw not only the genesis of the *Sonnets* and the completion of the *Elegies*, but also the arrival of a further twenty-five poems which seem, as one would expect, to belong to the 'family' of the *Sonnets*. During the same period Rilke found time to write the 'Brief des jungen Arbeiters' (the highly controversial 'Worker Letter') and also some substantial private letters, including three to Lou Andreas-Salomé.

The return to his work on the *Elegies* had meant that, initially at least, Rilke had had to retrace his steps and to undertake a kind of day-dream journey to the point in his past life at which that work had been abandoned. The image of the traveller pausing and turning to scan the landscape which has already been left far behind him occurs arrestingly in the Eighth Elegy. But here in the *Sonnets* there is preponderantly the sense of something different at work, the feeling that we are hearing the voice of a Rilke who suddenly finds himself, perhaps to his own surprise, standing in the very centre of his own and the world's living present and gazing around him; sometimes in dismay but also often in delight at being himself alive and living in that present, in that world. The *Sonnets* possess a special openness and lightness, a wind blows through them and their air is fresh to breathe. In the *Neue Gedichte*, too, the young Rilke under the example of Rodin had started to look at the things, animals and people in the world outside himself with a new freshness, a new surprise, and to make poetry from his looking: an immensely introverted young artist who had at last learned the trick of looking out *from* the self. In the *Sonnets* something similar is happening: Rilke seems again to succeed, this time in a slightly different way, in escaping from and transcending the closed box of *self*. It is as if the Singing God had handed him a key.

Both the *Elegies* and the *Sonnets* are difficult poetry, though they are not impenetrably so. Rilke's *Neue Gedichte* seem incomparably more accessible but there is no reason why we should not value one kind of poetry for its clarity and another, equally, for its mysteries. In the final year of his life, Rilke wrote to his publisher Anton Kippenberg asking to be sent copies of the *Elegies* and the *Sonnets* interleaved with plain paper, so that he could work on an interlinear text – to the *Sonnets* in particular – for his own use and for the use of certain of his friends. Rilke came only gradually to understand the difficulties presented by the *Sonnets* and to realise that there are lines in them that are almost incomprehensible without the help of some exegesis. And yet Rilke's own discursive commentaries can make the poetry seem even more hermetic than before – often his explanations are like prose-poems in their own right, and difficult prose-poems at that.

It is best to stay cautious in 'explaining Rilke'. In his first letter of 1903 to Franz Xaver Kappus, the officer-cadet 'young poet', the twenty-seven-year-old Rilke wrote to his nineteen-year-old disciple: 'there is nothing which touches works of art so little as does the language of criticism...Few things are in fact as accessible to reason or to language as people will generally try to make us believe. Most phenomena are *unsayable*, and have their being in a dimension which no word has ever entered; and works of art are the most unsayable of all – they are mysterious presences whose lives endure alongside our own perishable lives...' In a later letter he returned to this theme: 'Works of art are infinitely solitary, and nothing comes so little near them as does criticism. It is love alone that can grasp them and hold them and do them justice.'

Having entered Rilke's caveat, I shall nevertheless again grasp the nettle. Rilke's *Sonnets* are built around the Orpheus legend already taken up by him in the magnificent 'Orpheus. Eurydike. Hermes' of the *Neue Gedichte*. The story of Orpheus is perhaps based on the life of an actual historical figure, that of a Thracian follower of the cult of Dionysus. According to the legend he married Eurydice, a Dryad or tree-nymph, who was later bitten by a serpent and died. Orpheus valiantly descended to the Underworld to intercede for her return to the land of the living, and by his music so charmed Pluto and Persephone, the guardians of Hades, that they were persuaded to release her. But a condition was imposed that Orpheus should not look at his wife during the journey from Hades back to the world above. Orpheus, momentarily forgetting the prohibition, turned during the journey and looked at Eurydice. Thereupon Eurydice was banished forever to the Underworld; eternally lost to Orpheus by a moment's inattention on his part.

In the end Orpheus was attacked and torn to pieces by the Thracian Maenads. One explanation provides motive for the murder by claiming that he had interfered with the women's worship; another says that it was the revenge of the women for the embittered misogyny of the singer since he had been deprived forever of his Eurydice. In versions of the legend, the head and lyre of Orpheus proved indestructible and the head, still speaking, floated down the river Hebrus to be buried finally at Lesbos. According to Aeschylus and Euripides the charm of the song of Orpheus was so potent that it drew trees, wild beasts, and even rocks into its spell.

The Orphic legend later grew into a religion which gained adherents and took root in Attica and the south of Italy in the sixth and seventh centuries. The *Oxford Classical Dictionary* provides this summary:

> Orpheus is connected with Apollo; he is even sometimes said to be his son. The reason is that both laid stress on purifications and righteousness. Orphism implies legalism of ritual and life, mysticism of cult and doctrine, a speculative cosmogony and an anthropogony which emphasised the mixture of good and evil in human nature; it contributed to the transformation of the Underworld into a place of punishment. It made the individual in his relation to guilt and retribution the centre of its teaching...In the classical age it was despised; only Pindar and Plato understood its great thoughts. It sank down to rise again with the recrudescence of mystic ideas in a later age.

Vera Ouckama Knoop, the daughter of acquaintances of Rilke's, to whom the *Sonnets* are dedicated as a memorial, died of leukaemia during 1919. She was nineteen years old when she died. Rilke had seen her dance when she was little more than a child and he had been impressed and moved by her talent. Vera's mother, Gertrud Knoop, later sent Rilke an account of her daughter's fatal illness which he read in 1922 on the first day of the new year. By a tragic symmetry, Rilke himself was also to die of a leukaemia which, bafflingly, had not been diagnosed by his doctors until a month before his death on 29 December 1926. The theme of 'those who die young' had long been of special concern to Rilke, as evidenced in several of the *Elegies* and also in his three Requiem poems: for the painter Paula Modersohn-Becker; for Wolf von Kalkreuth, a young poet who had committed suicide at the age of nineteen; and for the nine-year-old Peter Jaffé.

The *Sonnets to Orpheus* are fundamentally poems of invocation, however successfully they may sometimes masquerade as 'discourse'. As we read them it becomes ever clearer that Rilke in part identifies with Orpheus, while the figure of Vera merges with that of Eurydice, among the Shades. Keeping company with these identifications is Rilke's celebration of the semi-divine Orpheus in his eternal vocation as originator of *song*, open-mouthed, inspired, indestructible, his singing head and still-sounding lyre surviving the stoning and tearing of the Maenads. For 'song' we may read 'art', the currency in which Rilke believed absolutely and to which he devoted his life with steadfastness and courage. It is not for nothing that Rilke's elegiac poetry is often found to be commemorative of artists and it is worth wondering if the narcissistic and terrible angels of the *Duino Elegies* do not perhaps represent the artists whose monomania and narcissism can at times seem both more and less than human. Rilke had had exceptional opportunities to study artist-monsters when he stayed at the artists' colony at Worpswede, and especially perhaps during the many fragile months in which he acted as secretary to Auguste Rodin, at Meudon.

The *Elegies* are dedicated to Marie Taxis, the *Sonnets* inscribed as a memorial to the young Vera. The story of the young dancer and the details of her illness and death were certainly among the elements from which the *Sonnets* grew, but neither Vera's story nor the Orpheus legend alone seems to lie at the heart of the *Sonnets* in any straightforward or literal fashion. Perhaps the *Sonnets to Orpheus* are charged above all with the poet's own thirsty curiosity about the nature of destiny, of a human life, whether Vera's short life or that of Rilke's friend Paula Modersohn-Becker or, indeed, his own relatively short life. Perhaps there is a special wish to understand the ways in which destiny might become even more complex and extended when it is the destiny of 'a dancer' or of 'a singer' – for there the *Doppel-*

bereich has to take on yet another dimension, and 'experience' has to work both for itself and for much more than itself.

Of the form of the *Sonnets*, Rilke wrote:

> I keep always referring to them as sonnets. They are perhaps the freest and most transfigured verse that might be understood as belonging to this form – usually so quiet and consistent. But it was the very task of transforming the sonnet, of picking it up and, as it were, taking it along on the run, without destroying it, that was in this instance my particular problem and my project.

The rhyming-schemes here differ little from those of the *Neue Gedichte* of fourteen years before, of which many are sonnets or near-sonnets. Rilke often switches from abba to cdcd, or from abab to cddc, in the octaves. The sestets contain either two or three rhymes. Rilke makes free use of the permutations permitted by these ground rules, but his rhymes fit with deadlock accuracy. In his metre he allows himself greater freedom, but none that by present-day standards would seem over-indulgent. There are tetrameters, pentameters, some hexameters and, very rarely, fourteeners. His rhythms are predominantly trochaic or dactylic and there are a number of long-liners that pick up and echo the rhythms of the *Duino Elegies*. Six sonnets, all in Part 1, make use of ultra-short lines which Rilke has borrowed from the French Symbolists. Rilke's rhythms support the content as well as carrying the sheer sound and movement of his poetry; nowhere more so than in the *Sonnets to Orpheus*. Part of the *Auftrag* of translation here might be to make lines that move in a manner that respects Rilke's own pace and ear.

One should not make too much of the many apparent similarities between *Elegies* and *Sonnets*. It is probably almost inevitable that similar language, similar images, should occur again and again across the two works – and this seems especially so when we reflect on the galloping pace at which this poetry was written. There is a misleading sense of familiarity in reading the *Sonnets* for one who already knows the *Elegies*, and vice versa:

their language, language in the deeper sense, is to some extent the same. But there is less reliable cross-elucidation given than one might expect, and the two works in the end reveal that they are less interconnected than they seem at first. Eudo Mason has suggested that we are justified 'in considering the *Sonnets to Orpheus* as quite distinct from the *Duinese Elegies* and in going in some respects beyond them'. It is a difference of ends where the means are often strikingly alike. To compare *Elegies* with *Sonnets* is interesting and rewarding – but it will not prove enormously helpful in 'discovering' the poems. What will invariably give such help is to read the poems; then to allow them a little time to settle; then to read them again. Conversely, Rilke's lines can remain stubbornly reticent if one tries to wring meaning out of them as one wrings out washing.

It would be a misjudgement to believe that the *Sonnets* are in any way 'less' than is the great project of the *Duino Elegies*. Although some of them are slight, although a few of them may seem underworked, there is a wonderfully accurate congruity between Rilke's own innocent, circumspect, complex, and endlessly paradoxical nature and the image, presented by legend and folklore, of the Singing God. The Orpheus material is as if heaven-made for Rilke: 'Orpheus. Eurydike. Hermes' in the *Neue Gedichte* seems already charged with the lyric conviction triumphantly present in the *Sonnets*. The *Sonnets* are far lighter in tone than the *Elegies*, the outward as against the inward stroke of Rilke's pendulum, diastole against systole, lyrical, and on the whole affirmative in comparison with the predominantly more oppressive and gothic *Elegies*. Part 1 of the *Sonnets* keeps something of the mood of the *Neue Gedichte* of 1907 and 1908, while Part 2 contains poetry closer to the *Elegies*; closer thematically, in complexity, and in the occasional difficulties of interpretation. But no sooner has this observation been made than the many exceptions to it come into sharp focus.

Although Rilke himself regarded the *Elegies*, too, as poetry of affirmation, they begin with a cry in the wilderness and their final image is one of descent – *wenn ein Glückliches fällt*. The *Sonnets* begin with the 'tall tree in the ear' and conclude with World as we know it from the Book of Genesis, our own planet with its stable land and its moving waters.

The *Duino Elegies* have been described as 'a project of being'. Such a project may have been what Rilke himself intended but is not necessarily the dimension in which the work has most to offer. The voice of the *Sonnets*, too, changes from invocation to legend and sometimes to homily. As moralising, preaching, there is matter that must seem contradictory or inconsistent, and even some that may be found offensive. Rilke is infinitely to be valued as a poet: as a preacher, too, he can be brilliant – but he is far less reliable in that role. However, a poem truly a poem (*in Wahrheit singen...*) will always contain more than can be preached and more than can be explained – both more and less than any overt message – so that poetry to some extent stays independent even of its own propaganda.

Works of art, as well as being 'infinitely solitary' (which might also mean 'self-complete'), can find their form and even their content partly through chance. It is a wonderful and teasing truth that poetry's power of invocation, its music, story, images, illuminations, *everything* of real importance, may be owed to the relatively unimportant conventions of rhythm or rhyme. What seems profoundly true of Rilke is that the best of this poet is to be found in the stuff of the poetry; in the nature of its language and of something almost beyond language, its fabric, cadences and imagery, sound and progression. Not discourse. Mystery.

STEPHEN COHN

Sonnets Part One

Sonnette Erster Teil

I

Da stieg ein Baum. O reine Übersteigung!
O Orpheus singt! O hoher Baum im Ohr!
Und alles schwieg. Doch selbst in der Verschweigung
ging neuer Anfang, Wink und Wandlung vor.

Tiere aus Stille drangen aus dem klaren
gelösten Wald von Lager und Genist;
und da ergab sich, daß sie nicht aus List
und nicht aus Angst in sich so leise waren,

sondern aus Hören. Brüllen, Schrei, Geröhr
schien klein in ihren Herzen. Und wo eben
kaum eine Hütte war, dies zu empfangen,

ein Unterschlupf aus dunkelstem Verlangen
mit einem Zugang, dessen Pfosten beben, –
da schufst du ihnen Tempel im Gehör.

I

A tree rose up – O apogee of rising!
Now Orpheus sings, all hearing's tallest tree.
And nothing speaks but signals in the silence,
new births and transformations, come to be.

From nests and earths deep in the melting wood
the silence and its creatures hastening here
stay hushed not out of cunning, not from fear
but eagerly to hear what must be heard.

No impulse now to bellow, howl or roar
and no roof there to shelter such a horde.
Where nothing but the merest refuge was,

answering only to the blackest need,
a tunnel entrance propped by trembling spars –
you built them their own Temples of the Ear!

II

Und fast ein Madchen wars und ging hervor
aus diesem einigen Gluck von Sang und Leier
und glänzte klar durch ihre Frühlingsschleier
und machte sich ein Bett in meinem Ohr.

Und schlief in mir. Und alles war ihr Schlaf.
Die Bäume, die ich je bewundert, diese
fühlbare Ferne, die gefühlte Wiese
und jedes Staunen, das mich selbst betraf.

Sie schlief die Welt. Singender Gott, wie hast
du sie vollendet, daß sie nicht begehrte,
erst wach zu sein? Sieh, sie erstand und schlief.

Wo ist ihr Tod? Oh, wirst du dies Motiv
erfinden noch, eh sich dein Lied verzehrte? –
Wo sinkt sie hin aus mir?...Ein Madchen fast...

II

A girl, an almost-girl, she bade farewell
to all the twinned delights of song and lyre
and in spring-gauzes, half ethereal
she made herself a bed within my ear

and slept in me and all things were her sleep:
the spaces, meadows, tangible and real,
all trees I ever gazed on, every shape
and every wonder I myself could feel.

She slept the World – How, God of Song, did you
create her never to desire awakening?
Was she set here only to sleep, to dream?

Where is her death? Can you not find the theme,
her requiem, before your songs decay?
Almost a girl where does she drift away?...

III

Ein Gott vermags. Wie aber, sag mir, soll
ein Mann ihm folgen durch die schmale Leier?
Sein Sinn ist Zwiespalt. An der Kreuzung zweier
Herzwege steht kein Tempel für Apoll.

Gesang, wie du ihn lehrst, ist nicht Begehr,
nicht Werbung um ein endlich noch Erreichtes;
Gesang ist Dasein. Für den Gott ein Leichtes.
Wann aber *sind* wir? Und wann wendet *er*

an unser Sein die Erde und die Sterne?
Dies *ists* nicht, Jüngling, daß du liebst, wenn auch
die Stimme dann den Mund dir aufstößt, – lerne

vergessen, daß du aufsangst. Das verrinnt.
In Wahrheit singen, ist ein andrer Hauch.
Ein Hauch um nichts. Ein Wehn im Gott. Ein Wind.

III

A God can do it. Mankind cannot press
boldly through the narrow lyre and follow:
our nature is double – where the heart's ways cross
no-one can build a temple to Apollo.

To sing as you teach song needs no desire,
no courtship of something the heart
in its own time may finally acquire.
Singing is being. Easy for the God.

When might *we* be? When will he turn around
the earth and stars to face our mortal being?
Not this, young lover, though your love may force

your mouth to open wide to give it voice.
Forget how once you sang. True singing
is whispering; a breath within the God; a wind.

IV

O ihr Zärtlichen, tretet zuweilen
in den Atem, der euch nicht meint,
laßt ihn an eueren Wangen sich teilen,
hinter euch zittert er, wieder vereint.

O ihr Seligen, o ihr Heilen,
die ihr der Anfang der Herzen scheint.
Bogen der Pfeile und Ziele von Pfeilen,
ewiger glänzt euer Lächeln verweint.

Fürchtet euch nicht zu leiden, die Schwere,
gebt sie zurück an der Erde Gewicht;
schwer sind die Berge, schwer sind die Meere.

Selbst die als Kinder ihr pflanztet, die Bäume,
wurden zu schwer längst; ihr trüget sie nicht.
Aber die Lüfte...aber die Räume...

IV

O you tender ones – will you wander
in the gentle breath not breathed for you?
Your cheeks in passing put it asunder –
blowing as one wind when you pass through.

O you blessed ones, sanguine and hale,
you who seem born to the heart's own world,
let the smile behind weeping forever prevail –
a bow to all arrows; each arrow's gold.

Teach yourselves not to be fearful of sorrow,
offer it back to the weight of the Earth –
to the sheer weight of mountains and seas!

Trees that we planted as children now grow
into burdens too heavy to bear;
yet there are spaces, still there's the breeze…

V

Errichtet keinen Denkstein. Laßt die Rose
nur jedes Jahr zu seinen Gunsten blühn.
Denn Orpheus ists. Seine Metamorphose
in dem und dem. Wir sollen uns nicht mühn

um andre Namen. Ein für alle Male
ists Orpheus, wenn es singt. Er kommt und geht.
Ists nicht schon viel, wenn er die Rosenschale
um ein paar Tage manchmal übersteht?

O wie er schwinden muß, daß ihrs begrifft!
Und wenn ihm selbst auch bangte, daß er schwände.
Indem sein Wort das Hiersein übertrifft,

ist er schon dort, wohin ihrs nicht begleitet.
Der Leier Gitter zwängt ihm nicht die Hände.
Und er gehorcht, indem er überschreitet.

V

Build no memorial but let the rose
blossom each year according to his pleasure;
for this is Orpheus – each metamorphosis
as this thing, or as this. We need not measure

different names for him: all song is Orpheus
now and forever. Now near – now far again.
And if for some few days he can surpass
the rose's lifespan – how much has been given!

Although he awaits the parting anxiously
he has to fade from us to make us see.
He is already where we cannot pass

for every note of his exceeds our being.
His hands slip through the lyric fence, transgress.
His whole obedience rests in his excess.

VI

Ist er ein Hiesiger? Nein, aus beiden
Reichen erwuchs seine weite Natur.
Kundiger böge die Zweige der Weiden,
wer die Wurzeln der Weiden erfuhr.

Geht ihr zu Bette, so laßt auf dem Tische
Brot nicht und Milch nicht; die Toten ziehts –.
Aber er, der Beschwörende, mische
unter der Milde des Augenlids

ihre Erscheinung in alles Geschaute;
und der Zauber von Erdrauch und Raute
sei ihm so wahr wie der klarste Bezug.

Nichts kann das gültige Bild ihm verschlimmern;
sei es aus Gräbern, sei es aus Zimmern,
rühme er Fingerring, Spange und Krug.

VI

Is he, then, mortal? No: formed by both
living and dead realms those qualities grew!
One long-familiar with roots of the willow
grows skilled in weaving the osier, too.

Never at bedtime leave out on your table
the bread and the milk that might summon the Dead:
let *him* then conjure under soft eyelids
their visitations in everything visible.

Let rituals of magic with fumitory, rue,
be to him like other things lucid and true.
Nothing can cheapen, nothing diminish

the things that he judges fitting as image.
Whether from burial-places or dwellings
let him praise pitchers and buckles and rings.

VII

Rühmen, das ists! Ein zum Rühmen Bestellter,
ging er hervor wie das Erz aus des Steins
Schweigen. Sein Herz, o vergängliche Kelter
eines den Menschen unendlichen Weins.

Nie versagt ihm die Stimme am Staube,
wenn ihn das göttliche Beispiel ergreift.
Alles wird Weinberg, alles wird Traube,
in seinem fühlenden Süden gereift.

Nicht in den Grüften der Könige Moder
straft ihn die Rühmung Lügen, oder
daß von den Göttern ein Schatten fällt.

Er ist einer der bleibenden Boten,
der noch weit in die Türen der Toten
Schalen mit rühmlichen Früchten hält.

VII

To give praise! For praising, his high vocation,
he was wrought: bell-metal from mineral stillness!
His heart, O it is the ephemeral winepress
pressing the grape for Man's lastingest wine.

Dust cannot stifle his voice, cannot harm it.
Ripening in his compassionate south
when he is seized by some subject sublime
song becomes vineyard and berry and growth.

In the vaults where the king decays
praise will not let him disguise what is real
nor that the gods let shadows fall.

Steadfast among the messengers
far through the Gates of the Dead he bears
chalices heaped with fruits for praise.

VIII

Nur im Raum der Rühmung darf die Klage
gehn, die Nymphe des geweinten Quells,
wachend über unserm Niederschlage,
daß er klar sei an demselben Fels,

der die Tore trägt und die Altäre. –
Sieh, um ihre stillen Schultern früht
das Gefühl, daß sie die jüngste wäre
unter den Geschwistern im Gemüt.

Jubel *weiß*, und Sehnsucht ist geständig, –
nur die Klage lernt noch; mädchenhändig
zählt sie nächtelang das alte Schlimme.

Aber plötzlich, schräg und ungeübt,
hält sie doch ein Sternbild unsrer Stimme
in den Himmel, den ihr Hauch nicht trübt.

VIII

In the Realm of Praise alone walks Grief:
naiad of the source fed by our weeping
she guards our precipitation, keeping
watch that it still glistens on the cliff

where the altars, where the arches start.
See, her patient shoulders might suggest
she still feels herself the recentest –
youngest of the siblings of the heart.

Triumph *knows*. Yearning soon surrenders. Only
Grief is still a novice. All night long she
learns her lessons, numbering old sorrows.

All at once – inaccurate and artless –
she lifts a constellation of our voices
to the high heavens undimmed by her own breath.

IX

Nur wer die Leier schon hob
auch unter Schatten,
darf das unendliche Lob
ahnend erstatten.

Nur wer mit Toten vom Mohn
aß, von dem ihren,
wird nicht den leisesten Ton
wieder verlieren.

Mag auch die Spieglung im Teich
oft uns verschwimmen:
Wisse das Bild.

Erst in dem Doppelbereich
werden die Stimmen
ewig und mild.

IX

Only to him who dares take up the lyre
even in the realm of the Shades
shall it be granted in awe to aspire
to unendingly praise.

Only one who has dwelt with the Dead
and eaten the juice of their flower
earns and retains every sound that is heard
now and forever.

Though what reflects in the pool
grows indistinct as it flows:
Know what it shows!

Not till the reign of the Double-
Kingdom can every voice sound
everlastingly kind.

X

Euch, die ihr nie mein Gefühl verließt,
grüß ich, antikische Sarkophage,
die das fröhliche Wasser römischer Tage
als ein wandelndes Lied durchfließt.

Oder jene so offenen, wie das Aug
eines frohen erwachenden Hirten,
– innen voll Stille und Bienensaug –
denen entzückte Falter entschwirrten;

alle, die man dem Zweifel entreißt,
grüß ich, die wiedergeöffneten Munde,
die schon wußten, was schweigen heißt.

Wissen wirs, Freunde, wissen wirs nicht?
Beides bildet die zögernde Stunde
in dem menschlichen Angesicht.

X

Ancient sarcophagi, never forgotten,
once more I greet you! Purling along
since Roman days the jubilant water
flows and advances – a journeying song.

You who lie open wide as the eyes
of a young herdsman waking in summer,
filled with warmth, silence and hedgerow flowers
while round him enchanted tortoise-shells flutter:

all who were rescued from doubting – I greet you!
mouths finally open once more,
mouths that have long known the meaning of stillness.

Listen: do *we* know it, not know it?
Either way shapes the hesitant hour
pictured in every human face.

XI

Sieh den Himmel. Heißt kein Sternbild ‘Reiter’?
Denn dies ist uns seltsam eingeprägt:
dieser Stolz aus Erde. Und ein zweiter,
der ihn treibt und hält und den er trägt.

Ist nicht so, gejagt und dann gebändigt,
diese sehnige Natur des Seins?
Weg und Wendung. Doch ein Druck verständigt.
Neue Weite. Und die zwei sind eins.

Aber *sind* sie’s? Oder meinen beide
nicht den Weg, den sie zusammen tun?
Namenlos schon trennt sie Tisch und Weide.

Auch die sternische Verbindung trügt.
Doch uns freue eine Weile nun,
der Figur zu glauben. Das genügt.

XI

Study the starscape: is one star called *Rider*?
Since our curious pride derives from Earth?
And is there another, higher,
which controls and guides it, which it bears?

Is not the very sinew of our nature
to be first pricked by spur then held by reins?
Path, and diversion. But a touch explains.
New perspectives. And the two unite.

Or do they? Or is it neither's choice,
this path they travel as their common road?
Manger and table will not share a place;

even connections in the stars mislead.
But if for a little while it pleases us
to trust the pattern...would not that suffice?

XII

Heil dem Geist, der uns verbinden mag;
denn wir leben wahrhaft in Figuren.
Und mit kleinen Schritten gehn die Uhren
neben unserm eigentlichen Tag.

Ohne unsern wahren Platz zu kennen,
handeln wir aus wirklichem Bezug.
Die Antennen fühlen die Antennen,
und die leere Ferne trug…

Reine Spannung. O Musik der Kräfte!
Ist nicht durch die laßlichen Geschäfte
jede Störung von dir abgelenkt?

Selbst wenn sich der Bauer sorgt und handelt,
wo die Saat in Sommer sich verwandelt,
reicht er niemals hin. Die Erde *schenkt*.

XII

Hail to the principle that can unite us!
for we truly move in abstract ways
and the ticking footsteps of our watches
walk beside our individual days.

Though ignorant of our true places
yet our acts are relevant and real.
The antennae feel for the antennae
and the emptiness conceives…

sheerest Energy: music of the Powers!
Do not ordinary actions every day
keep all interruptions from you?

Even if the farmer frets and worries
how it is that seed translates to summers
he will never know. The Earth gives freely.

XIII

Voller Apfel, Birne und Banane,
Stachelbeere... Alles dieses spricht
Tod und Leben in den Mund... Ich ahne...
Lest es einem Kind vom Angesicht,

wenn es sie erschmeckt. Dies kommt von weit.
Wird euch langsam namenlos im Munde?
Wo sonst Worte waren, fließen Funde,
aus dem Fruchtfleisch überrascht befreit.

Wagt zu sagen, was ihr Apfel nennt.
Diese Süße, die sich erst verdichtet,
um, im Schmecken leise aufgerichtet,

klar zu werden, wach und transparent,
doppeldeutig, sonnig, erdig, hiesig –:
O Erfahrung, Fühlung, Freude –, riesig!

XIII

Gravid apple, pear, banana, gooseberry
tell of life and death within each human
mouth that tastes and learns them thoroughly.
Read your child's expression when it chews them:

something rapt from far away indeed.
Does your mouth grow speechless in its turn?
for in place of words the unforeseen
issues from the fruit – amazed and freed.

Try to speak of what we call an apple:
speak the sweetness which at first grows dense
but distils in our experience

into something lively, liquid, crystal-
clear; ambivalent; mortal; sunny; earthy:
an event, sensation, pleasure...prodigy!

XIV

Wir gehen um mit Blume, Weinblatt, Frucht.
Sie sprechen nicht die Sprache nur des Jahres.
Aus Dunkel steigt ein buntes Offenbares
und hat vielleicht den Glanz der Eifersucht

der Toten an sich, die die Erde stärken.
Was wissen wir von ihrem Teil an dem?
Es ist seit lange ihre Art, den Lehm
mit ihrem freien Marke zu durchmärken.

Nun fragt sich nur: tun sie es gern?...
Drängt diese Frucht, ein Werk von schweren Sklaven,
geballt zu uns empor, zu ihren Herrn?

Sind *sie* die Herrn, die bei den Wurzeln schlafen,
und gönnen uns aus ihren Überflüssen
dies Zwischending aus stummer Kraft und Küssen?

XIV

We pass our lives among flowers, vines and fruit;
they speak more than the language of the year.
Out of the darkness rises something bright
and manifest – perhaps it shows a flicker

of envy from the Dead who fortify
our Earth. What do we know of this?
Since long ago their part has been to bless
and lard our own clay with their honest marrow.

We only ask, is their gift offered gladly
or do they thrust at us these benefits
clenched in their fists, earned by their slavery?

Are they our masters, resting among roots,
willing to spare us, from their own excess,
this hybrid gift that's part brute force, part kiss?

XV

Wartet..., das schmeckt...Schon ists auf der Flucht.
...Wenig Musik nur, ein Stampfen, ein Summen –:
Mädchen, ihr warmen, Mädchen, ihr stummen,
tanzt den Geschmack der erfahrenen Frucht!

Tanzt die Orange. Wer kann sie vergessen,
wie sie, ertrinkend in sich, sich wehrt
wider ihr Süßsein. Ihr habt sie besessen.
Sie hat sich köstlich zu euch bekehrt.

Tanzt die Orange. Die wärmere Landschaft,
werft sie aus euch, daß die reife erstrahle
in Lüften der Heimat! Erglühte, enthüllt

Düfte um Düfte! Schafft die Verwandtschaft
mit der reinen, sich weigernden Schale,
mit dem Saft, der die glückliche füllt!

XV

Wait now – that flavour; so quick in fading!
Just enough music, feet tapping, some humming:
O you ardent girls, you silent young women,
dance the shape of the taste you have tasted!

O dance the orange (who would not remember?)
drowning in sweetness but struggling against it,
changing at once when you possess it
into your substance, delicious and tender.

O dance the orange, its sunnier landscape!
Throw it away and let its ripeness
glow in our northland, radiantly naked,

fragrance on fragrance! Come to agreement
with the chaste rind which tries to refuse you
the sweet juices which flow for the lucky.

XVI

Du, mein Freund, bist einsam, weil...
Wir machen mit Worten und Fingerzeigen
uns allmählich die Welt zu eigen,
vielleicht ihren schwächsten, gefährlichsten Teil.

Wer zeigt mit Fingern auf einen Geruch? –
Doch von den Kräften, die uns bedrohten,
fühlst du viele...Du kennst die Toten,
und du erschrickst vor dem Zauberspruch.

Sieh, nun heißt es zusammen ertragen
Stückwerk und Teile, als sei es das Ganze.
Dir helfen, wird schwer sein. Vor allem: pflanze

mich nicht in dein Herz. Ich wüchse zu schnell.
Doch *meines* Herrn Hand will ich führen und sagen:
Hier. Das ist Esau in seinem Fell.

XVI

Old friend; this loneliness seeks you out
because with every word and sign
we piece by piece make the World our own
(perhaps its most fragile and menacing part).

Can *we* point fingers at a smell…?
of all the forces by which we are threatened
you too know many; have met with the Dead
and have been startled by magic spells.

See: it is purely a case of receiving
patches and pieces in place of the whole.
To give help is not easy, do not, above all

plant me in your heart – who would grow there too swiftly.
But my Master's hand I shall guide and will tell:
Touch! it is Esau – his own hairy fell.

XVII

Zu unterst der Alte, verworrn,
all der Erbauten
Wurzel, verborgener Born,
den sie nie schauten.

Sturmhelm und Jägerhorn,
Spruch von Ergrauten,
Männer im Bruderzorn,
Frauen wie Lauten…

Drängender Zweig an Zweig,
nirgends ein freier…
Einer! o steig…o steig…

Aber sie brechen noch.
Dieser erst oben doch
biegt sich zur Leier.

XVII

Ancient, enmeshed in roots,
hidden and sleeping:
deepest and absolute
ancestor: well-spring.

Helmet and hunting-horn;
grey heads in judgement;
brothers' fierce argument;
lutes, their fine women!

Branch blocks the branch that strives,
none can rise higher.
Here's one!…Ascend, O rise!…

These will all fracture yet:
this one is tallest but
bends to the lyre.

XVIII

Hörst du das Neue, Herr,
dröhnen und beben?
Kommen Verkündiger,
die es erheben.

Zwar ist kein Hören heil
in dem Durchtobtsein,
doch der Maschinenteil
will jetzt gelobt sein.

Sieh, die Maschine:
wie sie sich wälzt und rächt
und uns entstellt und schwächt.

Hat sie aus uns auch Kraft,
sie, ohne Leidenschaft,
treibe und diene.

XVIII

Master, do you hear its
throbbing and thrumming?
lauded by heralds…
Progress is coming!

Nowhere that ears can
endure its commotion
and still the engine
expects our devotion.

Mark the machinery
spinning its vengeance –
how it deforms and how it lessens us!

Drawn from our own, its power
owes but one favour:
humbly to serve and impartially labour.

XIX

Wandelt sich rasch auch die Welt
wie Wolkengestalten,
alles Vollendete fällt
heim zum Uralten.

Über dem Wandel und Gang,
weiter und freier,
währt noch dein Vor-Gesang,
Gott mit der Leier.

Nicht sind die Leiden erkannt,
nicht ist die Liebe gelernt,
und was im Tod uns entfernt,

ist nicht entschleiert.
Einzig das Lied überm Land
heiligt und feiert.

XIX

Though World may change as fast
as billowing cloud,
all things manifest must
grow back to the age-old.

Beyond the drift, the waves,
wider and freer
your prelude still survives,
God of the lyre!

Love yet remains unlearned;
hardship prevails unseen;
still veiled, still unrevealed

how Death shall take us.
Song alone through the land
sanctifies, praises.

XX

Dir aber, Herr, o was weih ich dir, sag,
der das Ohr den Geschöpfen gelehrt? –
Mein Erinnern an einen Frühlingstag,
seinen Abend, in Rußland – , ein Pferd...

Herüber vom Dorf kam der Schimmel allein,
an der vorderen Fessel den Pflock,
um die Nacht auf den Wiesen allein zu sein;
wie schlug seiner Mähne Gelock

an den Hals im Takte des Übermuts,
bei dem grob gehemmten Galopp.
Wie sprangen die Quellen des Rossebluts!

Der fühlte die Weiten, und ob!
der sang und der hörte – , dein Sagenkreis
war *in* ihm geschlossen.
Sein Bild: ich weih's.

XX

What, Master, shall I dedicate
to you who teach all creatures listening:
my clear remembrance of a day
in spring in Russia, and its evening...?

From the village nearby the white horse, alone,
one foreleg held by a trailing tether,
to wander the meadow, the night, on his own.
How the long, curling mane danced on his withers

to the beat of his cantering pride
and in spite of the halting pace
how the well-springs of horse-blood flowed!

Oh how he felt, was inspired by space,
sang, heard, *was* your song through
and through.
I dedicate this image to you.

XXI

Frühling ist wiedergekommen. Die Erde
ist wie ein Kind, das Gedichte weiß;
viele, o viele... Für die Beschwerde
langen Lernens bekommt sie den Preis.

Streng war ihr Lehrer. Wir mochten das Weiße
an dem Barte des alten Manns.
Nun, wie das Grüne, das Blaue heiße,
dürfen wir fragen: sie kanns, sie kanns!

Erde, die frei hat, du glückliche, spiele
nun mit den Kindern. Wir wollen dich fangen,
fröhliche Erde. Dem Frohsten gelingts.

O, was der Lehrer sie lehrte, das Viele,
und was gedruckt steht in Wurzeln und langen
schwierigen Stämmen: sie singts, sie singts!

XXI

Spring has come back again. The Earth is
like a child that's got poems by heart;
so many poems, so many verses,
patient toil winning her prizes at last.

Strict, the old teacher. We loved the whiteness
in the old gentleman's beard, its bright snows.
Now when we ask what the green, what the blue is,
Earth knows the answer, has learned it. She knows.

Earth, you're on holiday, lucky one: play now!
Play with us children! We'll try to catch you.
Glad, joyous Earth! The gladdest must win.

Every lesson the old teacher taught her,
all that is printed in roots and laborious
stems: now she sings it. Listen, Earth sings!

XXII

Wir sind die Treibenden.
Aber den Schritt der Zeit,
nehmt ihn als Kleinigkeit
im immer Bleibenden.

Alles das Eilende
wird schon vorüber sein;
denn das Verweilende
erst weiht uns ein.

Knaben, o werft den Mut
nicht in die Schnelligkeit,
nicht in den Flugversuch.

Alles ist ausgeruht:
Dunkel und Helligkeit,
Blume und Buch.

XXII

We are the strivers.
Yet Time's stride hastening
on is but paltriness
within the Unchanging.

All of that hurrying
must soon be gone:
all that's enduring
our prime commission.

Boys: don't burn courage
in striving for speediness;
don't yearn for flight.

Every thing bides at rest,
petal and printed page,
darkness and light.

XXIII

O erst *dann*, wenn der Flug
nicht mehr um seinetwillen
wird in die Himmelsstillen
steigen, sich selber genug,

um in lichten Profilen,
als das Gerät, das gelang,
Liebling der Winde zu spielen,
sicher schwenkend und schlank, –

erst wenn ein reines Wohin
wachsender Apparate
Knabenstolz überwiegt,

wird, überstürzt von Gewinn,
jener den Fernen Genahte
sein, was er einsam erfliegt.

XXIII

O not until Flight does more
than spread wings wide to please
private desires and soar
to a high silence of skies

like a bright cut-out to glide
or like the trick that succeeds
wooing the wind with display,
elegant, wheeling at ease –

not till the question of *why*,
what new machines might achieve,
outpaces puerile pride

shall he who reaches those heights
nearing that far-offness *be*
all that, alone, he must fly.

XXIV

Sollen wir unsere uralte Freundschaft, die großen
niemals werbenden Götter, weil sie der harte
Stahl, den wir streng erzogen, nicht kennt, verstoßen
oder sie plötzlich suchen auf einer Karte?

Diese gewaltigen Freunde, die uns die Toten
nehmen, rühren nirgends an unsere Räder.
Unsere Gastmähler haben wir weit –, unsere Bäder,
fortgerückt, und ihre uns lang schon zu langsamen Boten

überholen wir immer. Einsamer nun aufeinander
ganz angewiesen, ohne einander zu kennen,
führen wir nicht mehr die Pfade als schöne Mäander,

sondern als Grade. Nur noch in Dampfkesseln brennen
die einstigen Feuer und heben die Hämmer, die immer
großern. Wir aber nehmen an Kraft ab, wie Schwimmer.

XXIV

Shall we renounce our ancient friends the Gods? –
powerful, undemanding, but unknown
to the unyielding steel we fiercely breed.
Will we require new maps to track them down?

Those potent friends: they take from us our Dead
yet shun all contact with our turning wheels.
We have removed the baths and banquet halls
they used to use: their far too tardy

messengers we soon run down. In these days
we are lonelier and helpless in the hands
of other people, total strangers to us.

We build the new roads straight: no sweet meanders.
Our only fires drive the great steam-hammers.
And we decline in strength like failing swimmers.

XXV

Dich aber will ich nun, dich, die ich kannte
wie eine Blume, von der ich den Namen nicht weiß,
noch *ein* Mal erinnern und ihnen zeigen, Entwandte,
schöne Gespielin des unüberwindlichen Schreis.

Tänzerin erst, die plötzlich, den Körper voll Zögern,
anhielt, als goß man ihr Jungsein in Erz;
trauernd und lauschend – . Da, von den hohen Vermögern
fiel ihr Musik in das veränderte Herz.

Nah war die Krankheit. Schon von den Schatten bemächtigt,
drängte verdunkelt das Blut, doch, wie flüchtig verdächtigt,
trieb es in seinen natürlichen Frühling hervor.

Wieder und wieder, von Dunkel und Sturz unterbrochen,
glänzte es irdisch. Bis es nach schrecklichem Pochen
trat in das trostlos offene Tor.

XXV

You who were known to me, you like the flower whose name
guards its mystery, and who were ravished away –
once again I must recall and proclaim you,
graceful familiar of the unconquerable cry.

First as a dancer until her hesitant figure
was halted – like youth itself cast into bronze; alert,
motionless, grieving. Sent by those highest achievers,
Music descended and entered her transient heart.

Sickness walked near her. Already mastered by shadow,
already darkened, her blood raced into spring-time
swiftly outdistancing any suspicion.

Manifest ever again in hard setbacks and sorrow
it shone as if earthly. Then after terrible beating
entered the gate irremediably open.

XXVI

Du aber, Gottlicher, du, bis zuletzt noch Ertöner,
da ihn der Schwarm der verschmähten Mänaden befiel,
hast ihr Geschrei übertönt mit Ordnung, du Schöner,
aus den Zerstörenden stieg dein erbauendes Spiel.

Keine war da, daß sie Haupt dir und Leier zerstör',
wie sie auch rangen und rasten; und alle die scharfen
Steine, die sie nach deinem Herzen warfen,
wurden zu Sanftem an dir und begabt mit Gehör.

Schließlich zerschlugen sie dich, von der Rache gehetzt,
während dein Klang noch in Löwen und Felsen verweilte
und in den Bäumen und Vögeln. Dort singst du noch jetzt.

O du verlorener Gott! Du unendliche Spur!
Nur weil dich reißend zuletzt die Feindschaft verteilte,
sind wir die Hörenden jetzt und ein Mund der Natur.

XXVI

To the last, Godly one, you stay forever the singer.
When at the end the scorned rabble of Maenads beset you,
valiant one, you outsang their cries with your music.
Mobbed by destroyers, you raised the sweet order of song!

Not one among them could shatter your head or your lyre,
for all their furious striving; every sharp stone
flung at your heart when it touched was immediately turned
to a softness – and gifted with hearing.

But they finally tore you apart, those maddened avengers,
while yet the sound of you lingered in lions and boulders,
lingered in birds and in trees, where you sing still today.

Only because you were butchered in terrible anger
– O you lost God! O divine, indestructible trace! –
are *we* ears that can hear and a mouth for what Nature can say.

Sonnets Part Two

Sonnette Zweiter Teil

I

Atmen, du unsichtbares Gedicht!
Immerfort um das eigne
Sein rein eingetauschter Weltraum. Gegengewicht,
in dem ich mich rhythmisch ereigne.

Einzige Welle, deren
allmähliches Meer ich bin;
sparsamstes du von allen möglichen Meeren, –
Raumgewinn.

Wie viele von diesen Stellen der Räume waren schon
innen in mir. Manche Winde
sind wie mein Sohn.

Erkennst du mich, Luft, du, voll noch einst meiniger Orte?
Du, einmal glatte Rinde,
Rundung und Blatt meiner Worte.

I

Breath, you unseeable poem,
ceaselessly, freely exchanging
a measure of World for our being!
Counterpoint, of whose rhythm I *am*.

Singular wave! through increase
I am your gradual ocean,
thriftily guarding each portion;
husbanding Space.

So many regions in Space have been
harboured within me; many a wind
feels like a son to me.

Air that I breathe, filled with places once mine,
do you still know me? You, who were rind,
leaf and fruit of the words that I cry?

II

So wie dem Meister manchmal das eilig
nähere Blatt den *wirklichen* Strich
abnimmt: so nehmen oft Spiegel das heilig
einzige Lächeln der Mädchen in sich,

wenn sie den Morgen erproben, allein, –
oder im Glanze der dienenden Lichter.
Und in das Atmen der echten Gesichter,
später, fällt nur ein Widerschein.

Was haben Augen einst ins umrußte
lange Verglühn der Kamine geschaut:
Blicke des Lebens, fur immer verlorne.

Ach, der Erde, wer kennt die Verluste?
Nur, wer mit dennoch preisendem Laut
sänge das Herz, das ins Ganze geborne.

II

On any nearby scrap of card might fall
the truest line drawn by the Master's hand –
just as sometimes a looking-glass may find,
unique and sacred, a young woman's smile

when she surveys the morning, all alone
or served perhaps by artificial light,
whose breathing daytime face will only show
that smile's reflection, its pale counterfeit.

What, long ago, could human eyes
glimpse in the fire's darkening coal?
Visions of life irretrievably lost.

Who knows what is lost from our Earth, from our past?
None but the singer who steadfast in praise
may sing the heart which inherits the whole.

III

Spiegel: noch nie hat man wissend beschrieben,
was ihr in euerem Wesen seid.
Ihr, wie mit lauter Löchern von Sieben
erfüllten Zwischenräume der Zeit.

Ihr, noch des leeren Saales Verschwender – ,
wenn es dämmert, wie Wälder weit...
Und der Lüster geht wie ein Sechzehn-Ender
durch eure Unbetretbarkeit.

Manchmal seid ihr voll Malerei.
Einige scheinen *in* euch gegangen – ,
andere schicktet ihr scheu vorbei.

Aber die Schönste wird bleiben, bis
drüben in ihre enthaltenen Wangen
eindrang der klare gelöste Narziß.

III

Mirrors! Can anyone honestly claim
to have revealed your essence, your purpose?
You who like sieves are constructed of space,
openings worked in the fabric of Time.

You, prodigal of the ballroom's vastness
where as if pacing the forest gloom
lustres like royal sixteen-pointers
float through reflected, inviolate rooms.

Sometimes you seem as if crowded with pictures
some of them passing directly inside,
others not chosen, advised to pass by.

But the loveliest woman will linger
before you: in the cheeks she turns slightly away,
transparent and guilt-free, Narcissus can play.

IV

O dieses ist das Tier, das es sicht gibt.
Sie wußtens nicht und habens jeden Falls
– sein Wandeln, seine Haltung, seinen Hals,
bis in des stillen Blickes Licht – geliebt.

Zwar *war* es nicht. Doch weil sie's liebten, ward
ein reines Tier. Sie ließen immer Raum.
Und in dem Raume, klar und ausgespart,
erhob es leicht sein Haupt und brauchte kaum

zu sein. Sie nährten es mit keinem Korn,
nur immer mit der Möglichkeit, es sei.
Und die gab solche Stärke an das Tier,

daß es aus sich ein Stirnhorn trieb. Ein Horn.
Zu einer Jungfrau kam es weiß herbei –
und war im Silber-Spiegel und in ihr.

IV

Behold the animal that never was!
Men did not know this, so that nonetheless
they loved it, loved its stance, the luminous eyes,
its gait, the snowy neck, its quietness.

Still it did not exist. Then brought about
by love the thing came true. Now it was here
its head erect, and they made space for it.
And in that space uncompromised and pure

was *being* paramount? So it was reared
on *possibility* instead of grain.
Fed by that nourishment a single horn

erupted from its brow. The unicorn!
In all its whiteness then it met a virgin,
entered her silvered glass, and entered her.

V

Blumenmuskel, der der Anemone
Wiesenmorgen nach und nach erschließt,
bis in ihren Schooß das polyphone
Licht der lauten Himmel sich ergießt,

in den stillen Blütenstern gespannter
Muskel des unendlichen Empfangs,
manchmal *so* von Fülle übermannter,
daß der Ruhewink des Untergangs

kaum vermag die weitzurückgeschnellten
Blätterränder dir zurückzugeben:
du, Entschluß und Kraft von *wieviel* Welten!

Wir Gewaltsamen, wir währen länger.
Aber *wann*, in welchem aller Leben,
sind wir endlich offen und Empfänger?

V

Flower-muscle, gradually opening
meadow-day to the anemone
for the heavens to fill its open lap
pouring daylight's loud polyphony

into petals flexed to *gather in*
ceaselessly into the flower-star:
sometimes overwhelmed by the profusion
so that sunset's signal to retire

finds you with the outstretched petals scarcely
able to retract around you – you,
epitome of countless worlds' belief!

Far more forceful, we endure much longer.
Shall we too in any lifetime ever
learn that we can open and receive?

VI

Rose, du thronende, denen im Altertume
warst du ein Kelch mit einfachem Rand.
Uns aber bist du die volle zahllose Blume,
der unerschöpfliche Gegenstand.

In deinem Reichtum scheinst du wie Kleidung um Kleidung
um einen Leib aus nichts als Glanz;
aber dein einzelnes Blatt ist zugleich die Vermeidung
und die Verleugnung jedes Gewands.

Seit Jahrhunderten ruft uns dein Duft
seine süßesten Namen herüber;
plötzlich liegt er wie Ruhm in der Luft.

Dennoch, wir wissen ihn nicht zu nennen, wir raten…
Und Erinnerung geht zu ihm über,
die wir von rufbaren Stunden erbaten.

VI

Rose, you enchantment enthroned! To the Ancients
you were a cup with plain, simple rim;
in our own time, inexhaustible subject and portent
grown to profuse unaccountable bloom.

In your abundance like layer on layer of garments
over a body made only of light:
but each single petal as if it discarded
clothes altogether, was naked by right.

Centuries long your perfume has whispered
to us what to call it, each redolent name
suddenly present, ephemeral as fame

and we still cannot name it. We no more than guess it.
Ever towards it drift back the memories
begged long ago of the biddable hours.

VII

Blumen, ihr schließlich den ordnenden Händen verwandte,
(Händen der Mädchen von einst und jetzt),
die auf dem Gartentisch oft von Kante zu Kante
lagen, ermattet und sanft verletzt,

wartend des Wassers, das sie noch einmal erhole
aus dem begonnenen Tod – , und nun
wieder erhobene zwischen die strömenden Pole
fühlender Finger, die wohlzutun

mehr noch vermögen, als ihr ahntet, ihr leichten,
wenn ihr euch wiederfandet im Krug,
langsam erkühlend und Warmes der Mädchen, wie Beichten,

von euch gebend, wie trübe ermüdende Sünden,
die das Gepflücktsein beging, als Bezug
wieder zu ihnen, die sich euch blühend verbünden.

VII

Flowers: finally akin to the hands that will tend
(girls in the present, the long-ago past),
sprawled on the terrace-table end to end
bruised and exhausted where they were cast,

waiting that water one last time might restore
and reprieve them from dying already begun;
once again to be raised by the sentient power
of fingers invisibly charged to sustain

and to aid you far more than you are aware
when you gradually come to yourselves in the vase
shedding the feminine warmth you were given;

like sinners fatigued and repentant now shriven
of the sad fault that your plucking incurs,
shared by your kindred: the girls in their flower.

VIII

Wenige ihr, der einstigen Kindheit Gespielen
in den zerstreuten Gärten der Stadt:
wie wir uns fanden und uns zögernd gefielen
und, wie das Lamm mit dem redenden Blatt,

sprachen als Schweigende. Wenn wir uns einmal freuten,
keinem gehörte es. Wessen wars?
Und wie zergings unter allen den gehenden Leuten
und im Bangen des langen Jahrs.

Wagen umrollten uns fremd, vorübergezogen,
Häuser umstanden uns stark, aber unwahr, – und keines
kannte uns je. *Was* war wirklich im All?

Nichts. Nur die Bälle. Ihre herrlichen Bogen.
Auch nicht die Kinder... Aber manchmal trat eines,
ach ein vergehendes, unter den fallenden Ball.

In memoriam Egon von Rilke

VIII

You, my own childhood's few, long-ago playmates:
shyly we met, shyly befriended each other
in gardens scattered behind city streets,
and like the lamb with its talking banner

spoke without speaking. If at times we chanced to be joyful,
how could our gladness be anyone's property?
Quickly it melted away in the traffic of people
and in lingering years of anxiety.

Carriages drove by and passed and ignored us;
we were surrounded by houses, imposing yet false.
Nothing acknowledged us. Was there anything real?

Nothing. Except for the ball in the games that we played.
Not even the children...Unless an ephemeral child stood
under the marvellous arc of the ball as it fell.

In memoriam Egon von Rilke

IX

Rühmt euch, ihr Richtenden, nicht der entbehrlichen Folter
und daß das Eisen nicht länger an Hälsen sperrt.
Keins ist gesteigert, kein Herz – , weil ein gewollter
Krampf der Milde euch zarter verzerrt.

Was es durch Zeiten bekam, das schenkt das Schafott
wieder zurück, wie Kinder ihr Spielzeug vom vorig
alten Geburtstag. Ins reine, ins hohe, ins torig
offene Herz träte er anders, der Gott

wirklicher Milde. Er käme gewaltig und griffe
strahlender um sich, wie Göttliche sind.
Mehr als ein Wind für die großen gesicherten Schiffe.

Weniger nicht, als die heimliche leise Gewahrung
die uns im Innern schweigend gewinnt
wie ein still spielendes Kind aus unendlicher Paarung.

IX

You who give judgement, do not award yourselves praise
because irons and the rack are not fashionable still.
Where among you beats the heart that sheer pity has raised?
Mercy is not shaped by spasms of will.

What we have given the scaffold over the years
it will surely give back to us: just as a child may
offer as gifts the toys of its previous birthday.
It is not like this that a God truly merciful enters

into the welcoming heart like a wide-open door.
He would come as a God, all in light and in power enduring,
so much more than a wind for the sails of the great and secure.

Nothing less than a tender, mysterious vision
quietly conquering our hearts from within,
like an infant at play, conceived of an infinite pairing.

X

Alles Erworbne bedroht die Maschine, solange
sie sich erdreistet, im Geist, statt im Gehorchen, zu sein.
Daß nicht der herrlichen Hand schöneres Zögern mehr prange,
zu dem entschlossenern Bau schneidet sie steifer den Stein.

Nirgends bleibt sie zurück, daß wir ihr *ein* Mal entrönnen
und sie in stiller Fabrik ölend sich selber gehört.
Sie ist das Leben, – sie meint es am besten zu können,
die mit dem gleichen Entschluß ordnet und schafft und zerstört.

Aber noch ist uns das Dasein verzaubert; an hundert
Stellen ist es noch Ursprung. Ein Spielen von reinen
Kräften, die keiner berührt, der nicht kniet und bewundert.

Worte gehen noch zart am Unsäglichen aus…
Und die Musik, immer neu, aus den bebendsten Steinen,
baut im unbrauchbaren Raum ihr vergöttlichtes Haus.

X

The machine will forever imperil all human creation
while it presumes to direct us instead of to serve.
Lost is the hand of the Master, its fine hesitation:
rational buildings nowadays ask to be made of

rigidly accurate cuts of identical stone.
Nowhere that we can escape it. In the deserted
factory, self-lubricating, self-serving, alone
it stands, omniscient, alive as the life-force incarnate;

at one resolve it designs, manufactures, destroys.
Our lives retain their enchantments; everywhere still
magical forces appear when we worship and gaze.

Words still continue to tiptoe past the Unsayable.
Music, ever renewed in inviolable Space
builds of precarious stones its celestial house.

XI

Manche, des Todes, entstand ruhig geordnete Regel,
weiterbezwingender Mensch, seit du im Jagen beharrst;
mehr doch als Falle und Netz, weiß ich dich, Streifen von Segel,
den man hinuntergehängt in den höhligen Karst.

Leise ließ man dich ein, als wärst du ein Zeichen,
Frieden zu feiern. Doch dann: rang dich am Rande der Knecht,
– und, aus den Höhlen, die Nacht warf eine Handvoll von bleichen
taumelnden Tauben ins Licht... Aber auch *das* ist im Recht.

Fern von dem Schauenden sei jeglicher Hauch des Bedauerns,
nicht nur vom Jäger allein, der, was sich zeitig erweist,
wachsam und handelnd vollzieht.

Töten ist eine Gestalt unseres wandernden Trauerns...
Rein ist im heiteren Geist,
was an uns selber geschieht.

XI

Many a decent and orderly precept has death at its root:
ever anxious to dominate, mankind stays hunter from
first to the last.
I who know little of snares or of nets cannot forget
strips of bleached sailcloth, hung in dark caves of the Karst.

Introduced silently, gently, as if it were to unfurl
a banner to celebrate peace – then when the lad shook it out
from the black night of the caves fluttered a handful of pale,
tumbling doves into daylight...
But even this is permitted.

No-one who sees this enacted need be wrung by compassion,
nor need the hunter: his alertness and competence win
no more than time and chance offer.

Killing is only one aspect of our itinerant sadness.
No spirit unburdened will shun
what we ourselves have to suffer.

XII

Wolle die Wandlung. O sei für die Flamme begeistert,
drin sich ein Ding dir entzieht, das mit Verwandlungen prunkt;
jener entwerfende Geist, welcher das Irdische meistert,
liebt in dem Schwung der Figur nichts wie den wendenden Punkt.

Was sich ins Bleiben verschließt, schon *ists* das Erstarrte;
wähnt es sich sicher im Schutz des unscheinbaren Grau's?
Warte, ein Härtestes warnt aus der Ferne das Harte.
Wehe –: abwesender Hammer holt aus!

Wer sich als Quelle ergießt, den erkennt die Erkennung;
und sie führt ihn entzückt durch das heiter Geschaffne,
das mit Anfang oft schließt und mit Ende beginnt.

Jeder glückliche Raum ist Kind oder Enkel von Trennung,
den sie staunend durchgehn. Und die verwandelte Daphne
will, seit sie Lorbeern fühlt, daß du dich wandelst in Wind.

XII

Seek transformation, O take delight in the flame
in which boastful manifestations of change must be burned;
the draughtsman who skilfully renders his Earth in its lifetime
finds most to admire in the sweep of the form where it turns.

What locks itself into permanence swiftly grows tired –
should it feel safe and protected in featureless grey?
Listen. The voice of the hardest is warning the hard.
Somewhere a menacing hammer is raised.

Knowledge herself knows the one who dares flow like a
wellspring,
guides him enraptured through what the gods have created,
things that may close in beginning or start with their end.

Each happy dimension is the child or the grandchild of *parting*
which it in wonder explores. And Daphne, the goddess
translated,
in all her senses grown laurel, wants you transformed to a wind.

XIII

Sei allem Abschied voran, als wäre er hinter
dir, wie der Winter, der eben geht.
Denn unter Wintern ist einer so endlos Winter,
daß, überwinternd, dein Herz überhaupt übersteht.

Sei immer tot in Eurydike –, singender steige,
preisender steige zurück in den reinen Bezug.
Hier, unter Schwindenden, sei, im Reiche der Neige,
sei ein klingendes Glas, das sich im Klang schon zerschlug.

Sei – und wisse zugleich des Nicht-Seins Bedingung,
den unendlichen Grund deiner innigen Schwingung,
daß du sie völlig vollziehst dieses einzige Mal.

Zu dem gebrauchten sowohl, wie zum dumpfen und stummen
Vorrat der vollen Natur, den unsäglichen Summen,
zähle dich jubelnd hinzu und vernichte die Zahl.

XIII

Anticipate every farewell. You must put it behind
you as this passing winter will pass.
Yet, among winters one winter will come so endless
that overwintering it proves that your heart can survive.

Share in her death with Eurydice. Ascend in your song
and in praise ever-ascending combine with the pure.
Be, among Shades here in the Realm of Declining,
a ringing glass until, ringing, you shatter.

Be! yet at the same time remember the code of not-being,
endless dimension for every inmost vibration;
see you fulfil it this once and once-only time.

To the things we make use of, to the whole shabby unspeaking
store supplied by rich Nature, surpassing addition,
gladly account your own self and cancel the sum.

XIV

Siehe die Blumen, diese dem Irdischen treuen,
denen wir Schicksal vom Rande des Schicksals leihn, –
aber wer weiß es! Wenn sie ihr Welken bereuen,
ist es an uns, ihre Reue zu sein.

Alles will schweben. Da gehn wir umher wie Beschwerer,
legen auf alles uns selbst, vom Gewichte entzückt;
o was sind wir den Dingen für zehrende Lehrer,
weil ihnen ewige Kindheit glückt.

Nähme sie einer ins innige Schlafen und schliefe
tief mit den Dingen – : o wie käme er leicht,
anders zum anderen Tag, aus der gemeinsamen Tiefe.

Oder er bliebe vielleicht, und sie blühten und priesen
ihn, den Bekehrten, der nun den Ihrigen gleicht,
allen den stillen Geschwistern im Winde der Wiesen.

XIV

Look at the flowers, keeping good faith with the world,
to whom we at destiny's margins presume to lend destiny.
Who can be sure they do not regret how they fade? –
for to be their regret is perhaps our own duty.

Things that are pining to fly we burden with ballast,
adding our selves to their load and exulting in weight:
to the Things of our World O we are envious tutors
for they happily dwell in a childhood that lasts.

Imagine one who brought Things into the innermost heart
of his sleep: from the depths he had shared in the night
would he not differently wake to a different day?

But if he stayed, as he might, flowers would blossom and praise
him, the converted, now become one of their kind,
silent as one of their siblings blown by the meadow wind.

XV

O Brunnen-Mund, du gebender, du Mund,
der unerschöpflich Eines, Reines, spricht, –
du, vor des Wassers fließendem Gesicht,
marmorne Maske. Und im Hintergrund

der Aquädukte Herkunft. Weither an
Gräbern vorbei, vom Hang des Apennins
tragen sie dir dein Sagen zu, das dann
am schwarzen Altern deines Kinns

vorüberfällt in das Gefäß davor.
Dies ist das schlafend hingelegte Ohr,
das Marmor-Ohr, in das du immer sprichst.

Ein Ohr der Erde. Nur mit sich allein
redet sie also. Schiebt ein Krug sich ein,
so scheint es ihr, daß du sie unterbrichst.

XV

O fountain mouth so generous and wide
telling unceasingly the one true tale!
You marble mask that hides the water's smile!
From sources in the distant countryside

the aqueducts commence their march: from there,
beginning where the Appenines begin,
they skirt the ancient burial grounds and bear
the message to your dark and weathered chin

from which it spills into the reservoir
below: your ever-sleeping ear of stone.
The words you speak in it are said forever:
Earth's ear at audience with herself alone.

If *you* should choose to dip a pitcher in
you interrupt a liquid conversation.

XVI

Immer wieder von uns aufgerissen,
ist der Gott die Stelle, welche heilt.
Wir sind Scharfe, denn wir wollen wissen,
aber er ist heiter und verteilt.

Selbst die reine, die geweihte Spende
nimmt er anders nicht in seine Welt,
als indem er sich dem freien Ende
unbewegt entgegenstellt.

Nur der Tote trinkt
aus der hier von uns *gehörten* Quelle,
wenn der Gott ihm schweigend winkt, dem Toten.

Uns wird nur das Lärmen angeboten.
Und das Lamm erbittet seine Schelle
aus dem stilleren Instinkt.

XVI

Ever torn asunder by our hands
still the God remains our healing-place.
Always we stay sharp to understand
while the God dwells carefree and dispersed.

Offerings which men may consecrate
to him are acknowledged and received
only in his staying quite unmoved
to await the indeterminate.

Those already dead may drink
from the source whose sound is plainly *heard*
not until the God assents and gives his signal.

To us, only noise is offered.
And the wise lamb craves its bell –
following a quieter instinct.

XVII

Wo, in welchen immer selig bewässerten Gärten, an welchen
Bäumen, aus welchen zärtlich entblätterten Blüten-Kelchen
reifen die fremdartigen Früchte der Tröstung? Diese
köstlichen, deren du eine vielleicht in der zertretenen Wiese

deiner Armut findest. Von einem zum anderen Male
wunderst du dich über die Große der Frucht,
über ihr Heilsein, uber die Sanftheit der Schale,
und daß sie der Leichtsinn des Vogels dir nicht vorwegnahm
und nicht die Eifersucht

unten des Wurms. Gibt es denn Bäume, von Engeln beflogen,
und von verborgenen langsamen Gärtnern so seltsam gezogen,
daß sie uns tragen, ohne uns zu gehören?

Haben wir niemals vermocht, wir Schatten und Schemen,
durch unser voreilig reifes und wieder welkes Benehmen
jener gelassenen Sommer Gleichmut zu stören?

XVII

Where, in what delightful ever-watered gardens,
borne on what trees, grown of what softly-dispetalled
calyces
do the exotic fruits of Consolation ripen? Delicacies
these, such as even you might chance on

fallen in the trodden meadow of your poverty.
Ever again you would marvel at the fruit,
at its size and soundness and the tender peel,
each time thankful that no feckless bird has robbed you of it

nor the envious worms from underground. Over-
flown by angels, strangely tended by slow, secret gardeners,
are there trees that bear for us, though not our own?

We, who are no more than shades and phantoms – do our hasty
actions, ripening and withering before our season,
never harm the summer's casual serenity?

XVIII

Tänzerin: o du Verlegung
alles Vergehens in Gang: wie brachtest du's dar.
Und der Wirbel am Schluß, dieser Baum aus Bewegung,
nahm er nicht ganz in Besitz das erschwungene Jahr?

Blühte nicht, daß ihn dein Schwingen von vorhin
umschwärme,
plötzlich sein Wipfel von Stille? Und über ihr,
war sie nicht Sonne, war sie nicht Sommer, die Wärme,
diese unzählige Wärme aus dir?

Aber er trug auch, er trug, dein Baum der Ekstase.
Sind sie nicht seine ruhigen Früchte: der Krug,
reifend gestreift, und die gereiftere Vase?

Und in den Bildern: ist nicht die Zeichnung geblieben,
die deiner Braue dunkler Zug
rasch an die Wandung der eigenen Wendung geschrieben?

XVIII

Dancer: O you translation of everything
fleeting into sheer movement: how you achieve it!
And that tree grown of motion, your last pirouette,
mastering, seizing the year as it passed on the wing!

Did not the crown in its stillness suddenly flower –
to the pulse and the swarm of your rhythms that lingered?
Was it not sunshine, was it not summer
issuing out from the warmth that you kindled?

And it bore fruit too, the tree of your rapture:
are not these things its inanimate harvest? – the pitcher
striped like a gourd, the vase even riper and richer?

And there are pictures: does not the drawing remain
of your dark eyebrows instantly captured
on the surface prepared by yourself in your turning?

XIX

Irgendwo wohnt das Gold in der verwöhnenden Bank,
und mit Tausenden tut es vertraulich. Doch jener
Blinde, der Bettler, ist selbst dem kupfernen Zehner
wie ein verlorener Ort, wie das staubige Eck unterm Schrank.

In den Geschäften entlang ist das Geld wie zu Hause
und verkleidet sich scheinbar in Seide, Nelken und Pelz.
Er, der Schweigende, steht in der Atempause
alles des wach oder schlafend atmenden Gelds.

O wie mag sie sich schließen bei Nacht, diese immer offene Hand.
Morgen holt sie das Schicksal wieder, und täglich
hält es sie hin: hell, elend, unendlich zerstörbar.

Daß doch einer, ein Schauender, endlich ihren langen Bestand
staunend begriffe und rühmte. Nur dem Aufsingenden säglich.
Nur dem Göttlichen hörbar.

XIX

Gold lives somewhere in the bank. Waited-on, pampered,
it lays claim to thousands of intimate friends. Meanwhile
that beggar, the blind man, is like a lost desert-isle
to even the least copper penny – is like dust hidden under the cupboard.

Money seems quite at home in the shops down the street:
we see that it dresses in furs and carnations and silk.
He, never speaking, appears to be caught
in Money's pause between breaths, both asleep and awake.

Even at night, can his wide-open hand never close?
Each morning destiny sends for it, daily
extends it: so shining, so wretched, infinitely frail.

Who will at last comprehend this unending persistence
and wondering, praise it? None but the singer can say it.
None but a God ever hears.

XX

Zwischen den Sternen, wie weit; und doch, um wievieles noch weiter,
was man am Hiesigen lernt.
Einer, zum Beispiel, ein Kind...und ein Nächster, ein Zweiter –,
o wie unfaßlich entfernt.

Schicksal, es mißt uns vielleicht mit des Seienden Spanne,
daß es uns fremd erscheint;
denk, wieviel Spannen allein vom Mädchen zum Manne,
wenn es ihn meidet und meint.

Alles ist weit –, und nirgends schließt sich der Kreis.
Sieh in der Schüssel, auf heiter bereitetem Tische,
seltsam der Fische Gesicht.

Fische sind stumm..., meinte man einmal. Wer weiß?
Aber ist nicht am Ende ein Ort, wo man das, was der Fische
Sprache wäre, *ohne* sie spricht?

XX

Between the stars, how huge the dimensions. Still vaster
by far are the distances here.
Take for example a child...then look at another:
how ineffably distant they are.

Then does our fate measure us by the measure of *being* –
so that it seems something foreign?
When a girl keeps aloof from the suitor she has her eye on –
who could count the dimensions between?

Everywhere distance. Nowhere the circle completed.
Look at the dish on the table so cheerfully laid,
at the fish, at their curious faces.

Who knows? Once we were taught to believe fish are speechless.
But if they could speak, might not their language be spoken
in some
place that was fishless – *without* them?

XXI

Singe die Gärten, mein Herz, die du nicht kennst; wie in Glas
eingegossene Gärten, klar, unerreichbar.
Wasser und Rosen von Ispahan oder Schiras,
singe sie selig, preise sie, keinem vergleichbar.

Zeige, mein Herz, daß du sie niemals entbehrst.
Daß sie dich meinen, ihre reifenden Feigen.
Daß du mit ihren, zwischen den blühenden Zweigen
wie zum Gesicht gesteigerten Lüften verkehrst.

Meide den Irrtum, daß es Entbehrungen gebe
für den geschehnen Entschluß, diesen: zu sein!
Seidener Faden, kamst du hinein ins Gewebe.

Welchem der Bilder du auch im Innern geeint bist
(sei es selbst ein Moment aus dem Leben der Pein),
fühl, daß der ganze, der rühmliche Teppich gemeint ist.

XXI

O sing, my heart, sing the gardens you know not – they are as
gardens poured into glass; clear, unattainable.
Water, roses of Isfahan, of Shiraz,
sing them, delight in them, all incomparable.

Prove, O my heart, prove you cannot live without them,
that their figs ripening now ripen for you,
that you too have dwelt in breaths between flowering
branches, in an air that has burst into view.

Do not make the mistake of fearing to suffer
some deprivation in having decided to *live*.
You are a silken thread woven in, part of the weave.

Whether your place in the pattern is this or that figure,
even depicting the pains of the innocent,
know the entire, the glorious carpet is *meant*.

XXII

O trotz Schicksal: die herrlichen Überflüsse
unseres Daseins, in Parken übergeschäumt, –
oder als steinerne Männer neben die Schlüsse
hoher Portale, unter Balkone gebäumt!

O die eherne Glocke, die ihre Keule
täglich wider den stumpfen Alltag hebt.
Oder die *eine*, in Karnak, die Säule, die Säule,
die fast ewige Tempel überlebt.

Heute stürzen die Überschüsse, dieselben,
nur noch als Eile vorbei, aus dem waagrechten gelben
Tag in die blendend mit Licht übertriebene Nacht.

Aber das Rasen zergeht und läßt keine Spuren.
Kurven des Flugs durch die Luft und die, die sie fuhren,
keine vielleicht ist umsonst. Doch nur wie gedacht.

XXII

O despite fate, what grand abundances!
Here – overflowing in fountains. There – we have
stone figures carved at keystones of great doorways
buttressing the balconies above.

O the bronze bell! see how it raises its cudgel
warning off the dullnesses of everyday –
and at Karnak the column, the one and the only,
outlasting temples almost eternal.

Nowadays all these immeasurables, these very ones,
merely speed past us as *hurry* – past the yellow horizons
of day into the dazzle of over-lit night.

But the frenzy disperses, leaves nothing behind.
Vapour-trails arcing the skies, and their begetters,
perhaps have their place. – A place in the mind?

XXIII

Rufe mich zu jener deiner Stunden,
die dir unaufhörlich widersteht:
flehend nah wie das Gesicht von Hunden,
aber immer wieder weggedreht,

wenn du meinst, sie endlich zu erfassen.
So Entzognes ist am meisten dein.
Wir sind frei. Wir wurden dort entlassen,
wo wir meinten, erst begrüßt zu sein.

Bang verlangen wir nach einem Halte,
wir zu Jungen manchmal für das Alte
und zu alt für das, was niemals war.

Wir, gerecht nur, wo wir dennoch preisen,
weil wir, ach, der Ast sind und das Eisen
und das Süße reifender Gefahr.

XXIII

Call me to your side to meet the hour
which will unremittingly oppose –
as when fawning dogs first press up close
only then to turn away from you

when you do reach out to them at last.
What's withdrawn like this is your true kingdom.
We are set free when we are dismissed
where we were most certain of our welcome.

Anxiously we seek to find a hold,
still too young for what must seem too old
but too old for what was never tried.

We do justice only where we praise
for we are the timber and the blade
and a ripening sweetness of unease.

XXIV

O diese Lust, immer neu, aus gelockertem Lehm!
Niemand beinah hat den frühesten Wagern geholfen.
Städte entstanden trotzdem an beseligten Golfen,
Wasser und Öl füllten die Krüge trotzdem.

Götter, wir planen sie erst in erkühnten Entwürfen,
die uns das mürrische Schicksal wieder zerstört.
Aber sie sind die Unsterblichen. Sehet, wir dürfen
jenen erhorchen, der uns am Ende erhört.

Wir, ein Geschlecht durch Jahrtausende: Mütter und Väter,
immer erfüllter von dem künftigen Kind,
daß es uns einst, übersteigend, erschüttere, später.

Wir, wir unendlich Gewagten, was haben wir Zeit!
Und nur der schweigsame Tod, der weiß, was wir sind
und was er immer gewinnt, wenn er uns leiht.

XXIV

How that desire grows shoots when we loosen the soil!
Practically no-one assisted the earliest explorers,
nonetheless townships grew up close to ravishing harbours,
pitchers were filled, nonetheless, with fresh water and oil.

What of the Gods? We plan and refine them through sketches,
only to have them destroyed by a truculent Fate.
Still they remain the Immortals so that we yet
listen to them who will, finally, listen to us.

Thousands of years old, our race, mothers and fathers
ever more full of the infant for whom we still wait –
destined at first to outgrow and later to shatter us.

We, everlastingly ventured, have so long to spare.
Only taciturn Death truly knows what we are
and knows how greatly he profits by leasing us out.

XXV

Schon, horch, hörst du der ersten Harken
Arbeit; wieder den menschlichen Takt
in der verhaltenen Stille der starken
Vorfrühlingserde. Unabgeschmackt

scheint dir das Kommende. Jenes so oft
dir schon Gekommene scheint dir zu kommen
wieder wie Neues. Immer erhofft,
nahmst du es niemals. Es hat dich genommen.

Selbst die Blätter durchwinterter Eichen
scheinen im Abend ein künftiges Braun.
Manchmal geben sich Lüfte ein Zeichen.

Schwarz sind die Sträucher. Doch Haufen von Dünger
lagern als satteres Schwarz in den Au'n.
Jede Stunde, die hingeht, wird jünger.

XXV

Listen: can you hear the first of the harrows
working? Again, men's rhythms are heard
in an Earth still retentive, all silent, whose energies
wait for the spring. Nothing seems tired,

you can sense what is coming: every thing
so often experienced as if now made new.
You could not possess what, in spite of the waiting,
for all of your eagerness, now possessed *you*.

Even the leaves of the oaks overwintered
at evening light take tints of the future.
Sometimes one breeze sends another a sign.

Dark are the hedgerows. Mountains of dung
darker than darkness brood over the pasture.
Every hour that passes grows ever more young.

XXVI

Wie ergreift uns der Vogelschrei…
Irgendein einmal erschaffenes Schreien.
Aber die Kinder schon, spielend im Freien,
schreien an wirklichen Schreien vorbei.

Schreien den Zufall. In Zwischenräume
dieses, des Weltraums, (in welchen der heile
Vogelschrei eingeht, wie Menschen in Träume –)
treiben sie ihre, des Kreischens, Keile.

Wehe, wo sind wir? Immer noch freier,
wie die losgerissenen Drachen
jagen wir halbhoch, mit Rändern von Lachen,

windig zerfetzten. – Ordne die Schreier,
singender Gott! daß sie rauschend erwachen,
tragend als Strömung das Haupt und die Leier.

XXVI

How the sound of a bird-cry moves us –
any strong voice first formed long ago!
But the children out there at their play
let their high voices pass by true cries;

cry the fortuitous! Into tucked-away
havens of Earth-space (entered by genuine
bird-calls as *we* enter our dreams) penetrate
– driven like wedges – the shrieks of the children.

What has become of us…? Freer than free,
kites that have torn from the kite-string, we
buffet about between Earth and the heavens

our laughter tattered and frayed at edges.
O Singing God! awaken these criers
to bear on their current your head and your lyre.

XXVII

Gibt es wirklich die Zeit, dic zerstörende?
Wann, auf dem ruhenden Berg, zerbricht sie die Burg?
Dieses Herz, das unendlich den Göttern gehörende,
wann vergewaltigts der Demiurg?

Sind wir wirklich so ängstlich Zerbrechliche,
wie das Schicksal uns wahrmachen will?
Ist die Kindheit, die tiefe, versprechliche,
in den Wurzeln – später – still?

Ach, das Gespenst des Vergänglichen,
durch den arglos Empfänglichen
geht es, als wär es ein Rauch.

Als die, die wir sind, als die Treibenden,
gelten wir doch bei bleibenden
Kräften als göttlicher Brauch.

XXVII

Does it exist, then, Time the Destroyer?
When must the peaceful citadel be broken down?
When shall this heart which gods will ever own
fall to the Demiurge to overpower?

Are we truly as fragile, as helpless
as our Destiny seems to imply?
Childhood itself, once so rooted in promises
must it stand tongue-tied finally?

Ephemerality's spectre
passes as if it were vapour
through those who naïvely receive.

For what we are, we the strivers
are valued still by the Powers:
part of the life the Gods live.

XXVIII

O komm und geh. Du, fast noch Kind, ergänze
für einen Augenblick die Tanzfigur
zum reinen Sternbild einer jener Tänze,
darin wir die dumpf ordnende Natur

vergänglich übertreffen. Denn sie regte
sich völlig hörend nur, da Orpheus sang.
Du warst noch die von damals her Bewegte
und leicht befremdet, wenn ein Baum sich lang

besann, mit dir nach dem Gehör zu gehn.
Du wußtest noch die Stelle, wo die Leier
sich tönend hob – ; die unerhörte Mitte.

Für sie versuchtest du die schönen Schritte
und hofftest, einmal zu der heilen Feier
des Freundes Gang und Antlitz hinzudrehn.

XXVIII

Drift here, drift there, young woman still half-child,
achieve the pattern of your dance; surpass
the mere arithmetic dull Nature wields
and for one fleeting instant touch the stars.

For Nature's ears knew little till they heard
the voice of Orpheus – which moved you so
that you now grow impatient when some tree
waits over-long to follow where you lead

into the selfsame music that you hear.
You still recall where once the singing lyre
first sounded out – the legendary core!

You practised to perfect each movement, eager
to bring your friend to turn his countenance
and guide his footsteps to the sacred dance.

XXIX

Stiller Freund der vielen Fernen, fühle
wie dein Atem noch den Raum vermehrt.
Im Gebälk der finstern Glockenstühle
laß dich läuten. Das, was an dir zehrt,

wird ein Starkes über dieser Nahrung.
Geh in der Verwandlung aus und ein.
Was ist deine leidendste Erfahrung?
Ist dir Trinken bitter, werde Wein.

Sei in dieser Nacht aus Übermaß
Zauberkraft am Kreuzweg deiner Sinne,
ihrer seltsamen Begegnung Sinn.

Und wenn dich das Irdische vergaß,
zu der stillen Erde sag: Ich rinne.
Zu dem raschen Wasser sprich: Ich bin.

XXIX

Silent friend of every farness, mark
Show each breath you breathe increases Space!
Let your ringing sound out from the dark
bell-tower rafters, nourishing a force

stronger in the end than all it feeds on.
What in life has caused you greatest pain?
Make yourself at ease with transformation:
when drink is bitter change yourself to wine!

In the wanton night-time may you find
at the senses' crossroads, magic power...
arcane purpose where they coincide.

And if earthly powers should forget you,
to the constant Earth say this: I flow!
Tell the rushing waters: I abide.

Bibliography

The following abbreviations are used in the references.

Br I, II	RMR. *Briefe*, 2 vols, Wiesbaden 1950
Br 1914–1921	RMR. *Briefe aus den Jahren 1914–1921*, Leipzig 1937
Br Kappus	RMR. *Briefe an einen jungen Dichter*. Letters to a Young Poet, translated by Stephen Cohn, see below
Br Lou	RMR und Lou Andreas Salomé. *Briefwechsel*, Zurich and Wiesbaden 1952
Br Muzot	RMR. *Briefe aus Muzot 1921–1926*, Leipzig 1935
Br Taxis	RMR und Marie von Thurn und Taxis. *Briefwechsel*, 2 vols, Zurich and Wiesbaden 1951
Br Verleger	RMR. *Briefe an seinen Verleger 1906–1926*, Leipzig 1934
Elegies	RMR. *Duino Elegies*, German text with English translation by Stephen Cohn, Manchester 1989
G 1953	RMR. *Gedichte 1906–1926*, Wiesbaden 1953
K	August Stahl. *Rilke-Kommentar zum lyrischen Werk*, Munich 1978
Malte	RMR. *Die Aufzeichnungen des Malte Laurids Brigge*, Leipzig 1927
Mörchen	Hermann Mörchen. *Rilkes Sonnette an Orpheus*, Stuttgart 1958
NG	RMR. *Neue Gedichte, New Poems*. German text with English translation by Stephen Cohn, Manchester 1992
SW	RMR. *Sämtliche Werke*, 5 vols, Insel-Verlag 1955–66.

E.M. Butler	*Rainer Maria Rilke*, Cambridge 1941
J.M. Cohen	*Poetry of this Age: 1905–1965*, London 1966
Michael Grant	*Myths of the Greeks and Romans*, London 1950
Michael Hamburger	*An Unofficial Rilke*, London 1981
H.E. Holthusen	*Rainer Maria Rilke, A Study of His Later Poetry*, tr. J.P. Stern, Cambridge 1952
Eudo C. Mason	*Lebensanhaltung und Symbolik bei Rainer Maria Rilke*, Weimar 1939
Eudo C. Mason	*Rilke*, Edinburgh and London 1963
Ovid	*Metamorphoses*, tr. Mary M. Innes, London 1955
Donald Prater	*A Ringing Glass: the Life of Rainer Maria Rilke*, Oxford 1986
RMR	*Selected Letters, 1902–1926*, tr. R.F.C. Hull, London 1988
RMR	*Sonnets to Orpheus*, tr. J.B. Leishman, London 1936
RMR	*Sonnets to Orpheus*, tr. M.D. Herter Norton, London and New York 1992
RMR	*The Letters of Rainer Maria Rilke and Princess Marie von Thurn und Taxis*, tr. Nora Weidenbruck, London 1958
Paul Valéry	*Poésies*, Paris 1936
Rex Warner	*Men and Gods*, London 1950

Notes

PART ONE

I The first Sonnet sets on the page many of the conventions that are especially Rilke's own and that will be found throughout the *Sonnets*: paradox; compression; multiplicity of meaning. Rilke makes generous use of nouns to name both the very abstract and the very concrete, substantial, presences of which he constructs his poetry.

Music, song, poetry and dance are the essential realm of Orpheus; not far away lies ordinary speech, 'saying'; and ordinary movement, 'going'. Farther off, but related to the hierarchy, is 'architecture'. Within Rilke's convention these are to a large extent interchangeable: all of them belonging to the Orpheus-World.

Übersteigen means to 'exceed' or to 'transcend': the *über* part of the verb here signifies both 'above' and 'beyond'. Also, Rilke's tree-of-song is placed literally in the ear, giving five O-sounds to his second line.

Tiere aus Stille drangen aus dem klaren / gelösten Wald: it can mean (and does in part mean) 'beasts made of silence'. At the same time, the animals are hastening from out of the stillness as much as they hasten from out of the forest.

The portmanteau paradox, the black and the white of the poem's contrast, lies in the juxtaposition of Song to Silence. The one is conditional on the other and they become near-equivalents.

The end of the Sonnet is not easy to unravel: *ein Unterschlupf aus dunkelstem Verlangen* gives the image of a mineshaft, a burrow, and stands for the tunnel of the ear. The next line, *mit einem Zugang dessen Pfosten beben*, 'with an entryway whose posts tremble', suggests a tunnel entrance and its timbers: pit-props for the mineshaft. The line contains an image of the ossicles (hammer, anvil and stirrup) which transfer sound-vibrations from the ear-drum to the inner ear and eventually to the auditory nerve and the hearing-centres of the brain. (Rilke's extraordinary essay 'Ur-Geräusch' shows that he had an interest in the apparatus of hearing and that he knew at least a little cranial anatomy;

see SW VI, 1083ff.) The word 'tympanum' is the hidden link that connects organs of hearing with classical architecture. *Pfosten* should also be understood as anticipating the pillars of the temple of the last line of the sonnet. A three-cornered-puzzle.

Orpheus with his lute made Trees,
And the Mountaine tops that freeze,
Bow themselves when he did sing.
To his Musicke, Plants and Flowers
Ever sprung; as Sunne and Showers,
There had made a lasting Spring.

Every thing that heard him play,
Even the Billowes of the Sea,
Hung their heads and then lay by.
In sweet Musicke is such Art,
Killing care, and griefe of heart,
Fall asleep, or hearing dye.

Shakespeare, *King Henry VIII*, III.i.3

II It would be natural to believe that the almost-girl of the first line is Vera herself, so that the second Sonnet of Part 1 brings together the Singing God and the young dancer to whom the *Sonnets* are a memorial. However, there is very strong evidence to suggest that the almost-girl in Rilke's ear is his own *anima*: the feminine principle and muse of his own psyche. The important poem 'Wendung' together with passages in various letters supports this view (see SW II, 82; K, 303). It is known that Rilke had attended lectures by Alfred Schuler on the parts played by *animus* and *anima* in the creative process. A late Rilke poem in French gives further support to the thesis:

C'est de la côte d'Adam
qu'on a retiré Eve:
mais quand sa vie s'achève,
où va-t-elle, mourant?

Adam serait-il son tombeau?
Faut-il, lorsqu'elle se lasse,
lui ménager une place
dans un homme bien clos?

'Printemps VII', SW II, 545–6

Rilke delights in packing double, triple or multiple strands of meaning into one apparently straightforward image. The 'almost-girl' of this, the second Sonnet of the cycle, finds an echo in the 'almost-child' of Sonnet XXVIII of Part 2, the penultimate Sonnet. There can be no doubt that *that* poem is addressed to Vera.

III The conflicted nature of human awareness, especially when compared with the rest of the animal kingdom, is a prime theme of this Sonnet as also of the Eighth Elegy (*gegenüber sein / und nichts als das und immer gegenüber*: *Elegies*, 66, 67). In addition, Rilke was ever preoccupied (as was W.B. Yeats, his contemporary) with what he saw as the irreconcilable conflicts between life and art.

The image of the lyre as a gate and of its strings as bars will soon occur again in Sonnet V of Part I.

Hermann Mörchen notes (p. 66) that in antiquity cross-road shrines were dedicated to sinister deities such as Hecate, and never to Apollo the lucid god of poetry and song, the god whom Orpheus serves. (See also 2: XXIX.)

In this Sonnet it seems (although one might interpret the text quite differently) that the poet is advising novice 'singers' that it is as unprofitable to force poetry as to attempt to thrust camels through the eyes of needles. 'For the God' song is easy, as natural as breath: we ourselves should not expect to achieve the mastery of art through persistence or even through the inspiration of sexual love. Nevertheless, in a letter of 14 May 1904 Rilke had taken pains to advise the 'Young Poet' Franz Kappus: 'it is clear that we were meant to stay with what is hard'. (It can be argued that it is not easy to be easy.)

Rilke himself was aware, as were his critics, that his early writing had been flawed by poeticising and by striving for effects (by 'courtship'?). He is perhaps preaching to himself as much as to to others.

'When might *we* be?' Saint-Exupéry once suggested an anti-Cartesian proposition: 'Sometimes I think and sometimes I am'.

A literal translation of the poem's final line might read: 'A breath about nothing. A wafting in the God. A wind.'

IV The appearance of a bow and arrow in this Sonnet gives a clue to its kinship with the First Elegy (*wie der Pfeil die Sehne besteht*: see *Elegies*, 22, 23).

The breath and winds of the first stanza have blown there from the last lines of the preceding Sonnet, but in this one they seem to stand for Destiny and not for Poetry, and for a Destiny not especially directed at human beings. The winds will at once reunite behind all who wander in them, rather as the Red Sea closed behind the Israelites in their flight from Egypt. The Sonnet is speaking to women in general (but probably to *young* women in particular), who are believed to be especially at home in the 'realm of the heart'.

The admonition not to fear sorrow matches one of the themes of the Tenth Elegy, in which Rilke advises us to value it as one of the seasons and places essential to our own proper experience of our own lives.

V *Errichtet keinen Denkstein* ('Raise no memorial tablet...'), the Sonnet's opening instruction to us, its readers, finds an echo in Rilke's bitter image of the *Leidstadt*, the City of Sorrow, in the Tenth Elegy, in which the poet gives voice to his dislike for the monumental masonry and pomp of cemeteries, for funerary architecture and sculpture.

In place of the weight and assertiveness of a headstone, Rilke offers us the delicacy and ephemerality of the rose. Roses were Rilke's own supremely-treasured symbol for things exalted or transcendent, whether in this world or in another. 'Die Rosenschale' is the final poem of the First Part of the *Neue Gedichte*, and Rilke's mysterious self-epitaph holds up a last, a funerary rose.

> Rose, oh reiner Widerspruch, Lust,
> Niemandes Schlaf zu sein unter soviel
> Lidern.
>
> SW II, 1851

There is some tautology in Rilke's stressing that it is the Singing God who is the God of Song, but he is saying much more than this: the wonder of the Rose (indeed all wonder and all things wondrous) is itself poetry, is itself song: *Ein fur alle Male / ists Orpheus wenn es singt.*

As in Sonnet 1: III Rilke shows us the lyre as a barrier (with the vertical strings seen as bars or as a palisade). The paradox of 'obedience through transgression' is a reminder that artistry may have a duty to bend or to break the rules of its art; as in *tempo rubato* in musical performance, where strict time-keeping may be overthrown for the highest musical reasons. 'Transgression' and 'transcendence' live close to the meaning of the Sonnet's final *überschreitet*, 'oversteps'.

The second, third and fourth stanzas all end with an *über*-verb.

VI The first four lines carry the reminder that the Singing God is both mortal and immortal: he dwells both in the terrestrial and the celestial realms, among the dead and among the living. This is how his craft and his insight have come to flower. The Eighth Elegy carries a quiet echo of this text in its image of an Etruscan sarcophagus: the dead man lies interred *in* his box, but he simultaneously rests (as if alive) comfortably upon the lid.

Willow trees have long had a symbolic connection with mourning and with the Underworld. The herbs fumitory (earth-smoke) and rue were thought to possess the power to summon the dead; as was a table set with food.

The poem 'Hetären-Gräber' in the *Neue Gedichte* includes a dazzling inventory of the possessions buried with the dead Hetaerae – 'praised' in that instance by Orpheus-Rilke.

VII The first stanza of Sonnet VII promises that although poets themselves live only briefly, the 'wine' of their poetry will survive as something incomparably longer-lasting.

The Singing God's vocation of praising carries an obligation to tell truth and not merely to flatter and beguile, and truth is that even the greatest of kings will in the end decay (*et in Arcadia ego*) and that the Gods send not only light but also the deepest darkness. Notwithstanding, the messenger-Orpheus will continue to bear his lyric and affirmative message to the very portals of death and beyond them.

Both *Elegies* and *Sonnets* move (as does the message of this individual Sonnet) between praise and lamentation, between the light and the dark. The *Sonnets* are in general much lighter than the *Elegies*, but there are exceptions. Praise, *rühmen*, is the goal that the poet never lost sight of, believing that this was the proper vocation of Orpheus in all his many seasons and manifestations. The *Elegies* (especially parts of the Third and the whole of the Fourth) reach down to plumb some of the depths explored by Rilke while trying to arrive at the summit, and demonstrate the hardships of the spiritual journey that he undertook – seeking at the end to arrive at a poetry of praise and affirmation. The expression of praise, of lamentation and of loss continues in the next two Sonnets.

VIII *Klage* is elsewhere translated as 'Lament' or as 'Lamentation' or as 'Threnody'. Rilke makes his most dramatic use of the concept of *Klage*, and of its personification, in the Tenth Elegy: there I translated it as 'Grief', which still seems to me an appropriate choice for sound and for sense.

Line 1 of the German is an imperative: it is in the Realm of Praise alone that Grief is *permitted* to wander.

Niederschlag has been translated by Leishman as 'precipitation' in the sense that a chemist uses the word ('the precipitation of solids'). However, weather-men use the word to mean 'rain', and Rilke has just cited 'the well-spring of weeping'.

schräg und ungeübt, in the last stanza, is the kind of comment that might be given by an unimpressed drawing-teacher. (See note to 2: XXVI.)

IX

> ...while the new bride was wandering in the meadows, with her band of naiads, a serpent bit her ankle, and she fell lifeless to the ground. The Thracian poet mourned her loss; when he had wept for her to the full in the upper world, he made so bold as to descend through the gate of Taenarus to the Styx, to try to rouse the sympathy of the shades as well. There he passed among the thin ghosts, the wraiths of the dead, till he reached Persephone and her lord, who holds sway over these dismal regions, the king of the shades. Then, accompanying his words with the music of his lyre, he said:
>
> 'Deities of this lower world...I beg you by these awful regions, by this boundless chaos, and by the silence of your vast realms, weave again Eurydice's destiny, brought too swiftly to a close.'
>
> Ovid, *Metamorphoses* (tr. Innes, 225)

Mohn means 'poppy' (but can also mean 'poppy-seed'): in this instance it stands for *Schlaf-Mohn*, *Papaver somniferum*, for the opium poppy and for its narcotic product.

X The first stanza has origins in the poem 'Römische Sarkophage' in the *Neue Gedichte* (NG, 68, 69). The earlier poem describes the sarcophagus (literally, 'flesh-eater') which has by now disposed of the body long-ago entrusted to it, and which now serves, purified, as a part of the city's aqueduct system. Sarcophagi were regularly used as troughs for fresh water and were sometimes placed end to end to form culverts.

Rilke's imagery sharply contrasts the funerary purpose of the stone containers with the pure, life-giving flow of the waters which will eventually sing through them. It is an indication that we are once again in the *Doppelbereich* of the Living and the Dead, Mortals and Immortals, the Light and the Dark.

The second part of the octave recalls an image from Rilke's autobiographical novel, *Die Aufzeichnungen von Malte Laurids Brigge*, in which Malte fantasises that he sees the Prodigal Son in the role of a young shepherd. Malte pictures him standing '...in the spirit-haunted shade at Alyscamps, his gaze following the flight of a dragonfly between tombs that stand as open as the graves of the risen dead' (*Malte*, Part II, 181).

The first part of the sestet seems to express Rilke's own euphoria at having emerged from the years of relative silence and loss of impetus between 1914 and 1922. (The lid has at last come off the box in which he was, for so long, immured!)

Wissen wirs, Freunde, wissen wirs nicht?
Beides bildet die zögernde Stunde
in dem menschlichen Angesicht.

Rilke had written of the war-years: 'always believing that it must come to an end, not understanding, not understanding, not understanding. *To not understand*: yes, that was my entire occupation during those years – I can assure you it was not an easy one!' (Br 1914–1921, 292). Turning between *schweigen* and *sagen*, *wissen* and *nicht-wissen*, the last stanza moves again into a double-domain, citing the magic hour of illumination-mixed-with-hesitation (which must also mean 'doubt'), the sureness-in-unsureness which gives the human face its human look, and frankly expresses our human predicament.

The two last lines offer alternative readings (the one a mirror-image of the other), in which the subject and object will easily change roles.

XI Alcar and Mizar, Eques Stellula, Horse and Rider: these are names for a double star within the constellation of the Great Bear. *Reiter* is also to be found among the list of names of the symbolic stars of the Tenth Elegy.

Herman Mörchen is inclined to believe that the Horse-and-Rider stars of this Sonnet belong to Rilke's own universe of symbols; that they owe little to conventional astronomy (Mörchen, 118–19).

The Sonnet shares some of the content of the Eighth Elegy and offers a similar view on the differences in consciousness between mankind and the rest of the animal kingdom.

Rilke's questions finally ask: does the symbolic horse at heart *want* to make the journey urged on it by the rider's spurs? (For horse and rider we can as well substitute: Mankind and the Angel, servant and master, the Song and the Singer.)

Weide is generally used to mean 'pasture' or 'grazing', but that in its turn also signifies the place at which the grazing beasts, the ruminants, feed. 'Manger' and 'table' belong to the same class of objects, making it worthwhile to point at differences between them.

XII 'Reality' is currency of the kind that we spend and are given when our own substantial bodies move about (with us!) in actual, tangible, spaces. Alongside that experience there *may* be the ticking clock, which is able to tell us how long the adventure took. But what the clock measures is infinitely more abstract than what our senses experience when we are walking in the garden.

In electricity or radio-waves we confront something less abstract than time (although, as is also true of time, we experience their effects far more straightforwardly than we can experience their *nature*).

Die Antennen fühlen die Antennen: Rilke's line gives an image of radio-transmitters and receivers in communication with one another. Simultaneously, we can imagine insects rubbing palp against palp for social or for sexual purposes.

> Weite Speicher der Kraft baut sich der Zeitgeist, gestaltlos
> wie der spannende Drang der er aus allem gewinnt.
>
> *Elegies*, 60, 61

As in these lines from the Seventh Elegy, Rilke characteristically greets the Machine Age with revulsion. Here, however, he chooses to see machine energy as akin to the energies of Nature herself: Nature, the mysterious, the generous; grower and ripener of crops and flowers.

XIII There is an easy and unforced connection with much of the content of the previous Sonnet, and there is a palindromic shape to the pairing of subjects which the two Sonnets have in common.

Nature's open-handedness and the mystery of summer ripening have now borne literal fruit at the first line of Sonnet XIII. The Sonnet at once resumes the previous poem's soliloquies on the nature and valency of *experience* and of our senses.

We may put fruits into our mouths, or words. Of the two, which is the more unexpected, the more concrete (the more real?).

To *speak* an apple: who can do this? A poet?

If we trust the resemblance betwen the two Sonnets, we may believe that Rilke is proposing *poetry* as an analogue to *der Geist der uns verbinden mag*, 'the principle that can unite us'.

The 'fruit-verse' from Valéry's 'Le Cimetière marin' was probably the inspiration behind Sonnet 1: XIII and it can help towards a deeper understanding of its meaning:

> Comme le fruit se fond en jouissance,
> Comme en délice il change son absence
> Dans une bouche où sa forme se meurt,
> Je hume ici ma future fumée,
> Et le ciel chante à l'âme consumée
> Le changement des rives en rumeur.

XIV Images of flower, fruit and harvest, themes of life and death, are here carried over from the previous Sonnets and permeate Sonnets XIV and XV.

The belief that the blood and bones of the dead are required to render the land fruitful for the living, that the most fertile vineyards and cornfields are to be found on the sites of the bloodiest battles, is present in many agrarian cultures.

Generally we have been brought up in the belief that the dead are content to relinquish their all and to furnish the inheritance of the living, and that they will include their blessing in the legacy. Is this truly so? Is there, too, a sense in which the living will always continue to be mastered by their dead?

The questions may also serve as metaphors for the running (ever-running) debate between 'innovation' and 'tradition', the past and the present.

XV 'I see a voyce; now will I to the chinke, / To spy and I can hear my Thisbies face...' (Shakespeare, *A Midsummer Night's Dream*, V.i)

Synaesthesia (the 'production of mental sense impression by stimulation of another sense', OED) has been claimed to be an essential factor both in the creation and in the experiencing of everything in art.

Sonnet XV concludes the group of Sonnets whose text recommends that we pay attention to what is *experienced*, and here includes our experience of fruits.

XVI Although the Sonnet is addressed to a dog it has not lost all connection with the set of poems which immediately precede it.

Rilke explains to the dog himself that whereas he, the dog, lives entirely on the basis of his direct experience (he reads the world with his nose), mankind has pre-empted a great deal of this world – though not perhaps the most trustworthy part of it – by means of words and symbols.

This is very like the First Elegy's *und die findigen Tiere merken es schon / daß wir nicht sehr verläßlich zuhaus sind / in der gedeuten Welt* (*Elegies*, 20, 21).

In addition we find echoes of imagery and ideas from the Eighth Elegy, and a continuation of the previous discussion of difference between 'horse' and 'rider' (Sonnet XI).

In lines 13 and 14, Rilke surprisingly marries classical legend to the Old Testament in attempting to place the hand of Orpheus upon the pelt of Esau. Even more strangely, in his later note to the poem Rilke reveals that he believes that it was Esau, not his envious younger brother Jacob, who 'changed skins' in order to achieve an inheritance (SW I, 772). It may be that the persona of Esau was chosen by Rilke largely to establish the dog as 'our hairy brother', and he may also have intended the implication that mankind, articulate and 'smooth', has cheated the beasts of their birthright. Even without Rilke's confusion of Esau for Jacob, his explanation seems less clear than the poem itself.

There is another dog poem, in Part Two of the *Neue Gedichte*, and it does give some assistance in understanding the Sonnet. Dogs to Rilke are as Houyhnhnms to Jonathan Swift – a 'better' kind of creature than mankind. But Swift's horse-men are essentially more successful than mankind at being the honourable, fair-minded, *civilised* creatures that men ought to be and usually are not. Rilke, on the other hand, sees dogs as better-because-simpler; more *real* than humans; more directly in touch with World and what lives in it than humans; more reliant on the touch and smell and taste and sound of things in their 'reading' of real happenings in a real universe.

The (unintended?) paradox is neither stated nor implied: this is that the god who has dominion over humankind's highly conceptualised relations with the world (through symbols and abstractions, through 'languages' that only sometimes touch our sense directly) is Apollo – who is in turn closely connected with much that Orpheus represents.

XVII

Mais dans leur nuit toute lourde de marbres,
Un peuple vague aux racines des arbres
A pris déjà ton parti lentement.

Valéry, 'Le Cimetière marin'

As with other short-lined poems among the *Sonnets*, this example owes its form to poems by the French Symbolists. Nevertheless it has a predominantly German flavour.

Rilke offers us the compressed image of a family tree (wood becoming coal? or gemstones?). First, like a poet–archaeologist, he leads us underground and shows us the long-dead, primal progenitor of the (unquestionably noble) clan. Above ground, we find other clan-members busy hunting, making war, legislating, quarrelling and breeding. The lute-shaped women are lute-shaped because they, too, have a vocation to fulfil.

It is the *lyric* shoot that is potentially the highest and is at the same time the most supple, so that it may bend to its own vocation and does not need to compete with its competing rivals.

There are precedents in late nineteenth- and early twentieth-century literature and theory for models of cultural progression-by-declension (if this is to be judged by conventional yardsticks) as, for instance, in Thomas Mann's family saga *Buddenbrooks*. The stereotype is that of the inheritor who is fated at last to pour whatever family wealth remains into the thirsty soil of 'art'.

In his letter of 23 December 1903 to Franz Kappus (the 'Young Poet'), Rilke praises the 'wise incomprehension' of children (poets?) in relation to 'position' and 'occupation' as these things are understood by grown-ups. The letter provides an insight into Rilke's intentions in this Sonnet, which also has a significant precursor in 'Der Letzte' in the *Buch der Bilder* of 1902 (SW I, 395).

August Stahl comments: 'The belief that he himself is the last scion of a noble family, summoned by his vocation as an artist, is an autobiographical constant in Rilke's poetry' (K, 175).

XVIII In Sonnets XVII, XVIII and XIX are found *der Alte*, *das Neue* and *zum Uralten*: the line from the antique to the modern in the end comes circling back to the archaic. The Sonnets form a little cluster of the short-liners which we will meet again in Sonnets 1: XXII and 1: XXIII.

The present Sonnet, together with parts of the Seventh Elegy, perhaps most famously expresses Rilke's anti-Modern bias. It is by now a truism that German Expressionist artists such as Heckel, Kirchner, Nolde and Schmidt-Rottluff were uneasily caught between their desire to be modern and their paradoxical appetite for the primitive. Various writers of the same period wagged warning fingers against the cultural consequences of scientism and the Machine Age.

In the case of Rilke, whose preferences tended towards 'simple' artefacts (castles and cathedrals?), he would certainly have preferred to live in an agrarian culture still structured by its nobility, peasantry and craftsmen – an older order but one that, in his own case, did not seem to need to include Christian belief.

Rilke did not 'improve' Muzot with electricity or with modern sanitation, but he was not too pure to enjoy riding in the automobiles of his aristocratic friends and patrons.

It is easy enough to instruct the machines that their duty is to serve, yet the instruction alone may achieve little. In a letter to his publisher describing a car-journey, Rilke wrote: 'The machine prevails, you belong to the machine, at night you lie in your bed as if you were a spare-part and you dream and imagine the things that a bolt might imagine' (Br Verleger, 149).

XIX This and the previous Sonnet are so intricately related that they might be read as one poem: the machine-din that begins 1: XVIII is answered and overcome by the Orpheus-song at the conclusion of 1: XIX.

Sonnet XVIII ends in charging the machine that its duty is to *serve*. Now Rilke moves on to consider *change* – but here is meant neither the transformations nor the metamorphoses to which we should aspire: change, here, stands for the over-rapid (can-means-must!) revolution brought by the Machine Age, by the *Neu-Zeit*. Rilke may in part be restating the proposition that social 'evolution' must be necessary and benign, whereas 'change' is more often than not harmful. But his concerns go beyond a desire for social or for cultural good health: they are directed at mankind's highest conceivable fulfilment and at the 'completion' of his spirit.

Although the mission of Orpheus is to praise and to affirm, the Singing God finds himself able to enthuse over the *Neu-Zeit* only after overcoming the gravest reservations.

A rejected poem whose polemical thrust is cruder and more pietistic than 1: XIX originally stood in place of the present 1: XXI:

O das Neue, Freunde, ist nicht dies,
daß Maschinen uns die Hand verdrängen.
Laßt euch nicht beirrn von Übergängen,
bald wird schweigen wer das 'Neue' pries.

Denn das Ganze ist unendlich neuer,
als ein Kabel und ein hohes Haus.
Seht, die Sterne sind ein altes Feuer,
und die neuern Feuer löschen aus.

Glaubt nicht, daß die längsten Transmissionen
schon des Künftigen Räder drehn.
Denn Aeonen reden mit Aeonen.

Mehr, als wir erfuhren, ist geschehn.
Und die Zukunft faßt das Allerfernste
ganz in eins mit unserm innern Ernste.

SW II, 135–6

XX At first sight this Sonnet seems no more related to its context than a leaf dropped into a current.

In May 1900 Rilke and Lou Andreas-Salomé travelled (for a second time) to Russia: one of the events of the tour was a visit to the peasant-poet Spiridon Drozhin at his village Nisovka, on the upper reaches of the Volga. The episode of the white horse took place in the nearby countryside and is also described (in rather different detail) in Lou's travel-diary.

In his letter to Lou of February 1922, Rilke writes: 'I wrote, *made* the horse...*how* I made him, to be an *ex voto* for Orpheus! – *What* is time? *When* is "the present"? Across all those years he leaped – with his absolute joyfulness – right into my wide-open senses' (Br Lou, 464–5).

For Rilke, as for Proust his contemporary, certain images remembered across long passages of time take on the importance of a sacrament and begin to seem a partial answer to the largest human questions.

The exclamatory *und ob!* at the end of line 12 seems malappropriate and it may be no more than a desperate rhyme for *Galopp*.

Sagenkreis: in Ovid's *Metamorphoses* the song-cycle of Orpheus was performed by him on a day three years after he had, for the second time, lost his Eurydice to the Underworld. Orpheus, seated in a cypress grove, is gradually surrounded by an audience of trees, of birds and of beasts. He sings to them, his text a chain of legends linked to one another: stories of Phoebus and Hyacinthus, Pygmalion and Galatea, Myrrha and Cinyras, Venus and Adonis, Atalanta and Hippomenes. The sequence concludes with the death of Adonis.

XXI This *Frühlings-Kinder-Lied* ('Children's Spring Song') replaces the rejected Sonnet beginning: *O das Neue, Freunde, ist nicht dies...*(see note to 1: XIX).

It has its origin in the months that Rilke spent in Ronda in the south of Spain in 1912 and 1913. Rilke had listened to the children's singing in the little convent-church at Ronda – 'this dance-rhythm, to an accompaniment of triangle and tambourine': he had no idea at all *what* they had been singing (SW I, 772).

The tone of voice in which the Sonnet speaks and sings is pitched to sound a little childlike, although not to the point of affectation.

'Roots' and 'stems' variously carry a number of additional meanings in music, mathematics, philology, grammar, ethnology and genealogy.

The Sonnet's mood has something in common with the Ninth Elegy, but it is also related to Sonnet XXV of Part 2. Rilke described it as 'a pendant to the Sonnet of the white horse': both poems brilliantly recreate events first experienced by the poet in a far-distant past and a faraway place.

XXII Both music and mood of Sonnet XXII owe much to Goethe's *Chorus Mysticus*, the epilogue to *Faust*:

Alles Vergängliche
Ist nur ein Gleichnis;
Das Unzulängliche
Hier wirds Ereignis;
Das Unbeschreibliche,
Hier ists getan;

Das Ewig-Weibliche
Zieht uns hinan.

Sonnets XXII, XXIII and XXIV are all linked together by the subject of *Neu-Zeit*. Furthermore, XXII and XXIII are so closely related in form and content that they too, like XVIII and XIX, can be seen as a single poem in two parts.

Stillness, quietness, inwardness; lastingness, timelessness, space: in Rilke's currency such words possess endless metaphysical significance.

The verb *treiben* here conjures up a tide of city-ants hastening (bowler-hatted, Magritted) to and from the city-workplace. But the word also means 'to strive', 'to force', 'to drive' – even to the point of force with which hammers drive nails. Consequently there is a connection with Sonnet 1: III in which the Singing God warns unequivocally that song can *not* be forced. Rilke, between the lines, is writing as much about the making of art as about technological frenzy: 'those long, slow, happenings which stand so utterly in opposition to the extraordinary upheavals of our own times. Yet, alongside the most rapid change, there will forever be slow, gradual, movements; events, indeed, of so extreme a gradualness that we are not able to experience their passing' ('Der Brief des jungen Arbeiters', SW VI, 112).

XXIII The first successful *Flugversuche* were undertaken by the Wright brothers, in 1903: the two brothers flew together. Rilke's aviator, on the other hand is obliged to be a lone flier. By 1909, the year of Blériot's and Henry Farman's successful attempts, solo flight was becoming relatively commonplace, but here again there is reason to believe that *Flug* stands not only for itself but, just as importantly, is meant to double as a metaphor for the making of poetry (which more or less *has* to be solo flight).

Knabenstolz, young male pride, here stands for the over-confidence of the machine.

In his early poetry, before the *Buch der Bilder* and the *Neue Gedichte*, Rilke was often judged by critics to possess an almost monstrous facility; a too-great, too-fertile, too-easy talent in the service of too little genuine substance. An air-display?

XXIV There is a little irony to be discovered within the sad sincerity of Sonnet XXIV, just as there is certainly some satisfaction in the nostalgia with which Rilke gazes back from the pea-soupers of the Age of Steam towards the clarity and light of classical antiquity, saluting its only-too-human gods.

If there is 'praise' to be found in this text, then it is certainly not praise of the status quo, of the *Neu-Zeit*.

> We can also see the increasing anonymity of life as the scale grew larger and larger...
>
> ...the full horror of the new bargain: the bargain by which in exchange for sustenance a man forgoes the right to have his existence noticed. No god invented by man has ever had the power to exact such punishment.
>
> John Berger, *The Success and Failure of Picasso*, London 1965, 61

XXV During the very last days of 1921, Rilke was sent by Vera's mother a painfully moving account of her daughter's long illness, ending in her death by leukaemia. He first began to read Vera's story on New Year's Day.

Vera, as her illness progressed, had turned her attention away from dance and towards music, and, later still, to drawing.

It is certainly by intention that Sonnet XXV is rhythmically and syntactically so complex, as if Rilke had meant in this way to recreate some of the young woman's pain and uncertainty.

The *glänzte es irdisch* of line 13 might refer back to *das Blut* in the previous stanza, but Rilke probably intended it to signify the anonymous *es* of the dark forces gathered around the by now helpless Vera.

XXVI

> ...a band of women, driven wild by their dancing in the mountains by night, and angry at being despised by him, swept down upon the divine singer and tore him limb from limb, scattering the fragments of his body far and wide throughout the fields of Thrace. As for his head, wrenched from the neck that was as white as marble, the river Hebrus carried it to the sea and across the sea to the island of Lesbos. And, as the head was rolled in the river's stream, the voice and cold tongue still cried: 'Eurydice, my poor Eurydice!' and the name Eurydice was echoed from the banks.
>
> Rex Warner, *Men and Gods*, 126

PART TWO

I *Atmen du unsichtbares Gedicht* was the last of the *Sonnets to Orpheus* to be written, and Rilke had originally placed it at the end of Part 2.

The Second Elegy contains a number of images which echo this Sonnet:

> Denn wir, wo wir fühlen, verflüchtigen; ach wir
> atmen uns aus und dahin...

And also:

> ...wir nur
> ziehen allem vorbei wie ein luftiger Austausch.
>
> *Elegies*, 26, 27

Nevertheless, in the Elegy our breathing is seen as loss, as entropy, while in the Sonnet it becomes pure alchemy – the base gases transformed into the precious metal of poetry and song!

Concepts of change, metamorphosis, transubstantiation; of 'air-y substitution', visibility into invisibility, corporeal into incorporeal, breath into word, artefact into memory, are central to Rilke's own beliefs concerning life and art.

In Sonnets I, II and III of Part 2, Rilke takes up subjects that are, if not indeed invisible, in one way or another insubstantial: breath, temporality, images in the mirror, looking-glass-space. (The next group, from 2: IV to 2: IX, will also deal with relatively abstract material.)

The tree-of-words here, at the end of the Sonnet, recalls the tree-in-the-ear of the beginning of the first Sonnet of Part 1.

Professor Werner Fuchs has suggested that in 'Früher Apollo', the first of the *Neue Gedichte*, Rilke may have added dimension to his first draft of the poem by substituting *Gedicht* for the more obvious *Gesicht* (the sculpture in question was a head, not a figure). The same may also have been true of Sonnet 2: I: *unsichtbares Gesicht* seems a possible Rilkean oxymoron.

II Here, the mirror-image of a smile is 'real', whereas the event itself may be a 'reproduction'.

The unforced, the unmeditated, unplanned, unforeseen, unrepeatable, unwatched, the unrewarded, the unadmired – this kind of currency is obliquely but enthusiastically evoked and praised by Orpheus-Rilke in the Sonnet.

The theme of looking-glass-worlds connects this poem to the next in the sequence, but there is also an underground connection with the theme of 'innocence': the unlearned, unforced singing of the God in Sonnet III of Part 1.

III The looking-glass of the previous poem now takes over to become the theme of Sonnet 2: III.

'Lustres': this word can stand for the cut-glass pendants of a crystal chandelier but it can also, as here, signify the chandelier itself.

A 'Royal' is a stag of twelve or more points. Elk or deer antlers were sometimes fixed together to form chandeliers for the great rooms of castles and country houses.

It is worth considering that although mirrors may be seen as doorways into an alternative space, it is only in ghost-stories that they can make adjustments to time. In a Rilke poem, 'Der Junggeselle', in the *Neue Gedichte*, it is left to the mirror to rearrange the room so as finally to reveal its attendant ghost.

Wherever there are 'reflections' in a Rilke poem, it may be that Narcissus will put in an appearance. (See also note to 2: XII.) There are three Narcissus poems by Rilke as well as two by Valéry with which Rilke was familiar; and he was probably much aware of the Narcissus in himself!

ihre enthaltenen Wangen – 'her withheld cheeks' – describes, I believe, the pose in which a woman may examine her own image in the glass.

IV The 'mirror' and the 'Narcissus' themes of the two previous Sonnets are resumed in this Sonnet: the symbolism of the poem is both more playful and more profound than it may seem at a first reading.

At the end of Part One of *Malte*, Rilke gives a description of the six tapestries of *La Dame à la licorne* in the Musée de Cluny. It ends: 'It is a looking-glass that she holds. Do you see? She is showing the unicorn its own image' (*Malte*, Part 2, 191).

The Sonnet's apotheosis, its white wedding, is not drawn in until the final lines of the sestet. Does sexual love always find its beginnings in narcissism, in the looking glass?

There is an important and much earlier unicorn-poem in Part I of the *Neue Gedichte* (NG, 62–5), as well as 'La Dame à la licorne', the Sonnet of the same period dedicated to Stina Frisell (G 1953, 200–1). Similarities and differences between Rilke's treatments of the subject show something of the manner in which his preoccupations had changed between 1905–6 and 1922. But the shift from a kind of life- or still-life-painting towards more inward or metaphysical concerns should not be over-stressed. Rilke's individual voice, his persona as a poet, holds a consistency already present in some of the earlier poems, of the *Stundenbuch* and of the *Buch der Bilder*, and continuing until the *Komm du, du letzter, den ich anerkenne*, the final entry in the last of Rilke's notebooks (SW II, 511).

The shining masculine beast of this Sonnet will be replaced in Sonnet 2: V by a feminine archetype: Rilke's wide-open anemone, endlessly hopeful and acceptant.

V 28 June 1914 saw the assassination of the Archduke Ferdinand and his wife at Sarajevo, followed by a sequence of declarations of war.

On the 20th, Rilke had sent Lou Andreas-Salomé a letter containing his just-completed poem 'Wendung' ('Turning-Point'). Between these two dates, another letter to Lou, of 26 June, contains the following:

> I am so like the little anemone I once saw in the gardens in Rome; it had opened itself up so wide in the course of the day that when night fell it was no longer able to close. It was quite shocking to see it so open in the darkened meadow, still avid to *take in* – into its frantically-wide-open chalice; swamped by the night above it – inexhaustible...I, too, am as irremediably turned outwards, and I am consequently distracted by everything, refusing nothing. My senses, altogether without my permission, make towards every disturbance: when there is noise, I give myself up and I *am* that noise – and since anything that is focused on stimulus *wants* to be stimulated, I clearly want to be disturbed, and am so, without end.
>
> Br Lou, 341–4 and 349–50

Rilke's genuine distress at having been cast by destiny in the role of 'receiver' shows in the letter to Lou. Nevertheless, the present Sonnet clearly sets out to praise this very kind of openness to all experience. (See also Sonnet 2: XXVII, which takes up the same theme but with an opposite bias.)

VI Rilke believed that the only rose known to Classical Antiquity was 'the simple eglantine', the sweet briar. He was mistaken in this belief.

The mysterious 'naming of the rose' has nothing to do with ordinary language or with Linnaean classification: it has everything to do with comprehension, with 'possession'. Naming, in this sense, implies power, and the rose guards its mystery, its anonymity, and eludes would-be possessors.

Themes of 'inwardness' and 'outwardness', 'reality' and 'appearance', proliferate throughout the *Sonnets*: when the rose has shed its petals, has undressed, what is seen is scarcely to be recognised as a rose. The 'body made only of light' may have been suggested by the ray-like filaments of the stamens.

'Scent' and 'memory' are closely connected: of all the senses, taste and smell may be the most powerful in their capacity to trigger 'recall'.

The Sonnet has similarities both with 'Das Roseninnere' and with 'Die Rosenschale' of the *Neue Gedichte*. (See also the note to 1: V.)

VII The three fruit-sonnets of Part 1 find their counterpart in the flower-sonnets of Part 2, of which this poem is the last. In it, Rilke constructs a fugue on the inter-relatedness of flowers and young women, but the Sonnet also has secondary themes of temporality and mortality. The sprawling wounded on the garden table and the attentions of the girls with their kind, warm hands and 'healing' pitchers of water might conjure the image of a war-time hospital, the starch-and-crackle of nurses' uniforms.

The sexual fate of the young women is compared to the fate of the flowers: it is implied that both are predestined for gathering, and both, it is curiously suggested, share in the sin that they must (passively?) endure.

The poem runs its course as one strange, single, invocation; parenthesis following parenthesis; the narrative ending more or less where it began – and at the Sonnet's only full-stop.

VIII In various medieval pictures there is a lamb bearing a ribbon or flag with a text, very like the speech-balloon convention of present-day strip-cartoons.

Childhood is the theme to which Rilke returns as faithfully as other poets return to love (in the wars of love, he was the soldier who finds it his *duty* to walk away from the battle). In the first of the letters to the young Kappus, he writes: 'Even if you were kept in a prison...would you not still possess your childhood...? And if poems should be born of this inwardness...you will see in them your own precious, appropriate inheritance, a piece of your own life which speaks with your own voice' (Br Kappus, 17 February 1903).

The poet took his own advice: in the *Neue Gedichte* alone there are more than ten poems in which childhood plays an important part. Although Rilke's various evocations of childhood experience in poetry and prose are sometimes weighted with sorrow and anxiety (children are not permitted, by natural circumstances or by society, to control their own lives, and may suffer bitterly in consequence), nevertheless Rilke generally seems to find a kind of happiness in the *recollection* of much that was sorrowful, painful or frightening in its own time.

Similarly, towns and cities (notably Prague, Paris, Rome, St Petersburg) inspired both excitement and revulsion in him. It was unquestionably Paris that he most loved and feared, and it was Paris that most ripened him as a poet. (But the most important part played in ripening a man often belongs to a woman rather than a city: in Rilke's case this was Lou Andreas–Salomé, a fact of which he was not unaware.)

Egon von Rilke, the poet's cousin, to whom the Sonnet is dedicated, died young and is also commemorated elsewhere: in *Malte*, in the Fourth Elegy, and in various letters.

The falling ball makes an appearance in two other poems: 'Der Ball' (NG 272, 273) and 'Solang du Selbstgeworfnes fängst' (SW II,132).

IX *Rühmt euch, ihr Richtenden*...This rather Savonarolan text is written, in praise only of what-might-be, by a poet unimpressed by humanitarian pretensions of the *Neu-Zeit*. Its mood has been anticipated by descriptions of loneliness, angst and alienation surrounding the city-children of the previous Sonnet. *Their* childhoods were passed in the 1880s, whereas the persistent barbarism that Rilke is preaching against here puts medieval racks and iron-maidens on exactly the same level as tanks and air-burst shells, wire and mustard-gas.

It is nearly but not entirely unnecessary to suggest that Rilke's text has grown even more relevant in the seventy-eight years since it was written.

Sonnet 2: IX was judged by Rilke himself to be among the most 'beautiful' (successful, rather?) of the entire canon (Br Lou, 469, 634).

Its argument is related by the subject of *Neu-Zeit* to the two Sonnets which follow. It is also connected to Sonnet 2: VIII by the image of 'catching the falling ball': this points openly towards a reaching-for-something transcendently above ourselves. At heart, what the Sonnet argues is that a social, a rational, a civic or *political* humanism is unequal to our needs: what *is* needed is an apotheosis, a sheer transcendence of all that until now has achieved nothing better than the 'humane'.

The 'infant' of the final line might be born of a union between what is human and what is divine: perhaps those ancient, anthropomorphic Gods of Sonnet 1: XXIV from whom the *Neu-Zeit* has unwisely apostasised.

Sonnet 2: IX is the first of a small group of Sonnets (2: IX–XIV) which are similar in one respect: in all of them the octave has material which is (whether mildly or deeply) disturbing, whereas the sestet presents a reassuring message or a joyfully exalted image; sunshine after storm.

X The Machine Sonnet of Part 2 is set at a point in the cycle roughly comparable with that of its counterpart, Sonnet 1: XVIII. *Dröhnen* has given way to *bedrohen*, and the very short lines of the Part 1 Sonnet have been replaced by long lines rich in dactylic feet.

In the older tradition of fine building, even the *Zögern*, the 'hesitation', of the master-craftsmen was a wonder – whereas the contemplative 'knocking', the handling, the chisel-marks, of the banker-mason have been replaced in the *Neu-Zeit* by an anonymous and numbing machine accuracy, and by the howling and the spray-and-sludge of machine-saws.

Certainly, all this seems to lie a long way from any possibility of 'praising', but then, in the sestet, Rilke's mood is transformed as he turns to consider human assets that seem (so far?) imperishable: 'words' that can gently approach (although they will never quite touch) the many things that will stay and must stay 'unsayable'. Words that 'go out' as does breath from the nostrils, the notes from the trumpet's bell. And even more exalted is *music* – our supreme and supremely functionless architecture.

The 'celestial house' of the last stanza is placed in absolute opposition to the *entschlossernen Bau* of the first. It is the cathedral at Chartres against the Gropius Model Factory at Cologne.

XI Rilke's own note to this puzzling Sonnet:

> It concerns the manner in which, in certain regions of the Karst, following ancient hunting practices, the curious, pale, rock-doves are scared out from their underground habitations – by carefully introducing cloths and then suddenly shaking them in a particular way – so that they can be shot as they fly out, frightened.
>
> SW I, 773

Gentle in manner, fastidious, hyperaesthetic, vegetarian, Rilke has constructed this Sonnet with a rhetorical bias that might seem to point directly away from its overt conclusion. Perhaps, too, the poem has more to offer as *poetry* if read as irony rather than as a truism from Doctor Pangloss ('what is, is what must be; we too have to die').

> As Flies to wanton Boyes, are we to th' Gods,
> They kill us for their sport.
>
> Shakespeare, *King Lear,* IV.i.36

XII There may be an intentional caesura between Sonnets XI and XII of Part Two, but if we can believe that Rilke intended a connection between *Wolle die Wandlung* and the strangely flat dictum at the conclusion of the previous Sonnet, then much is explained.

The Sonnet cites in turn the four elements: Fire, Earth, Water and Air.

The Ninth Elegy has:

> Between hammer and hammer it dwells
> and it beats, our own heart. As our tongue
> lives between its own teeth,
> and yet still continues in praise.
>
> *Elegies*, 74, 75

Rilke is often an enthusiast for various forms of deprivation: poverty; parting; death. This is by no means merely an ideological tic, for it has its roots in the belief that 'loss' may be the prelude to 'transcendence'.

There is a related poem entitled 'Abschied' in Part One of the *Neue Gedichte* and there is also a late poem in *Vergers* (SW I, 553):

> Tous mes adieux sont faits. Tant de départs
> m'ont lentement formé dès mon enfance.
> Mais je reviens encor, je recommence,

ce franc retour libère mon regard.

Ce qui me reste, c'est de le remplir,
et ma joie toujours impénitente
d'avoir aimé des choses ressemblantes
à ces absences qui nous font agir.

Daphne, pursued by the amorous Apollo, escaped from him by her own transformation into a laurel. *Abschied* is the concept by means of which the present Sonnet is coupled to the next in the cycle.

XIII *Partir, c'est mourir un peu.* The death that must be transcended here is no small death for it is the second, and in this case irremediable, death of Eurydice. This time, also, it is Orpheus himself who must bear the burden of reponsibility for the tragedy.

Death, Transformation, and now Parting-in-Death: the sequence of related themes is continued from the conclusion of the previous Sonnet. The heat of the last poem's transcendental flame is here answered by the cold of winter, and of a winter, moreover, that is never-ending: it is the cold season in which the Singing God must learn and transcend his bereavement.

Lines 9–12 take up a theme that occurs in Sonnets 1: VI and 1: IX: the *Doppelbereich* which is the dimension of being and of not-being, of the Living and of the Dead, inhabited by Orpheus himself.

Ein Mal jedes, nur ein Mal...: 'Only once...' This occurs, unforgettably, in the Ninth Elegy, where it is stressed and developed by many variant repetitions (*Elegies*, 70, 71). It is here echoed briefly but sharply in line 11 of the Sonnet.

The Fifth Elegy has:

Wo die vielstellige Rechnung
zahlenlos aufgeht.
(where the sum with its so-many figures
adds up to nothing at all.)

Elegies, 48, 49

This is very similar to the ending of Sonnet 2: XIII, but in the Elegy the image stands for nullity, whereas in the Sonnet it stands for abundance.

In a letter to Vera's mother enclosing this Sonnet, Rilke wrote: 'Today I send you only *one* Sonnet, because it is the closest to me of the whole collection and, in the end, the one that stands for most among them all' (Br Muzot, 133).

The final sequence of the *Sonnets* is, largely, the sequence in which they were written. It could be argued that it is the bitter leave-taking of Eurydice's return to the Underworld that calls up the very necessity for 'transformation', so that Sonnets 2: XII and 2: XIII might well have been transposed.

XIV

> And why take ye thought for raiment? Consider the lilies of the field, how they grow; they toil not, neither do they spin.
>
> Matthew 5: 28

> Le don de vivre a passé dans les fleurs!
>
> Valéry, 'Le Cimetière marin'

Sonnets 2: XII and 2: XIII stand as a watershed in the series: it is hard to identify the change that they initiate, a change in mood and in voice. From this point on, too, the poems will grow even freer and even more casually interconnected. Sometimes they seem more related to Rilke poems outside the cycle than to any within it. The present Sonnet, however, bears comparison with the previous flower-Sonnets (there will be no more of them) and especially with 1: V and 1: VII.

Sonnet 2: XIV must also be regarded as a *Ding-Gedicht*, a 'thing-poem'. In it, Rilke weighs 'consciousness' against 'openness' – the openness, for example, of the little anemone of Part 1.

The First Elegy has:

> ...nor to expect from roses – nor to expect
> from any thing of exceptional wonder – interpretation
> of Mankind's future...
>
> *Elegies*, 24, 25

In 'Requiem für eine Freundin', Rilke, in contemplating the rose placed upon his standing-desk, asks: 'What is *my* consciousness to *her*?' (SW I, 650). It is the self-unawareness of 'things' that is so enviable.

A conventional listing of hierarchy (in the sense of 'to whom and to what most respect is owed') would run downwards from adult humans (men before women), to children, to animals, and only finally to 'things'.

Rilke, for whom such a pecking-order might have been reversed, nevertheless maintained a special respect for 'tradition' and for the well-born among his friends, of whom there were many.

It may be a creative imperative for artists to seek to avoid pretension which can amount to a kind of untruthfulness (see Sonnet 1: VII). For a poet of Rilke's persuasion, poetry, however fanciful, must bear witness and must keep good faith. The still-lives (painted *Ding-Gedichte*?) as well as the portraits of Cézanne are among the great masterworks of unpretension and were vitally influential models to Rilke.

XV The fountain mouth 'inexhaustibly speaking one, pure thing' suggests the *Bocca della Veritá* of the Roman church of S. Maria in Cosmedin: this is the ancient mouth of a fountain, in which, according to the tradition, the Romans would place their right hand when taking an oath. If this was done in bad faith, the stone mouth would close in punishment.

> Lively and never-ending, the waters pass over the great aqueducts and flow into the city, into the many piazzas, dancing over the bowls of white stone, spreading to fill the generous width of the basins, they murmur by day and murmur more loudly by night; and night is immense and filled with stars and soft with breezes .
>
> Br Kappus, 29 October 1903

Two sonnets from the *Neue Gedichte* have furnished Rilke with much of the material for this poem: 'Römische Fontäne' provides the fountain itself, and 'Römische Campagna' gives its provenance: the mountains, the burial grounds, the aqueduct.

Significantly, the sound of the falling water, Earth speaking interminably to herself, may be 'interrupted' by a representative of mankind; but this can never lead to dialogue.

XVI The Sonnet begins with echoes of Sonnet XXVI of Part 1, that is, with the tearing of Orpheus by the Maenads: *scharf* and *verteilt* come directly from the earlier Sonnet, but what they now signify is not the same.

To 'await the indeterminate' must amount to waiting forever: what we come to the source to acquire is wisdom (we are 'sharp to understand') but what the god will provide is no more and no less than his sound, his music.

The 'sound of the source' is carried over from the last Sonnet and from its fountain, while the Earth conversing with itself (it is not quite the same thing as a monologue) now becomes merged with sounds that proceed from the strangely impassive Singing God: he can heal but can neither be bribed nor 'understood'. The sound of its bell, its own kind of music, tells the lamb where it finds itself; and no more. Its wisdom is to understand that so much, and no more, is its due.

XVII The 'singing source' of the previous Sonnet could provide water only for the dead. Here, the clear water flows in abundance. However, this Sonnet is most firmly related to the Persian Garden Sonnet (2: XXI) which it anticipates.

The theme of Consolation may specially come in answer to the novice Grief ('Lamentation') of Sonnet 1: VIII, as well as to the many themes of Grief-transcended which lie at the heart of the Sonnets – also intended, perhaps, for Vera's mother, Gertrud Ouckama Knoop.

A connection with the 'Fruit Sonnets' of Part 1 (XIII, XIV, XV) is plain but is not of great significance.

A 'slow, secret gardener' (he is both Destiny and Death) also appears as *der gärtnender Tod* in the 'Hero Elegy' (the Sixth), as does an image of self-anticipation, of 'being ahead of oneself'. Here the question is left open: *do* our precipitate actions harm or not harm the natural world?

The foolish birds and covetous worms of line 8 of the Sonnet, over-flying, under-burrowing, have been rapidly transformed by Rilke into the angels and gardeners of lines 9 and 10.

XVIII This is the second of only three Sonnets in which the poet speaks directly to Vera–Eurydice. The first stanza bears a similarity to the lines of the Fifth Elegy, the *Elégie des saltimbanques*, in which Picasso's boy-acrobat is apostrophised very much as Rilke here addresses the girl-dancer:

> Then you: falling a hundred times daily
> and bruising (still green!) from the tree
> grown of everyone moving together (the tree
> which swifter than water races its seasons;
> into mere minutes crams spring-summer-autumn)
> ...You land on the grave like a windfallen apple.
>
> *Elegies*, 46, 47

The Sonnet takes up the tree symbol of the very first poem of the series: the 'tree of sound' constructed by Orpheus is here replaced by the 'tree of movement' brought about by the dancer, by Vera herself.

There is also present the implied suggestion that 'art' and 'time' are metaphysically connected: the dancer's pirouette, at the same time movement and stasis, becomes the blossoming tree – it is as if the swarming of its bees were helping to hold it in magical suspension, out of time. 'Transience' itself, the fleeting movement, the fleeting year, are captured and transfixed by the concentration and talent of the whirling dancer: her pirouette is 'suspension'.

The image of the spinning girl gives birth to another image: the clay cylinder spinning on a potter's wheel; the vase; the pitcher.

In the final stanza, the outstretched arms of the pirouetting dancer, taken with the vertical of her spinning legs and trunk, describe the T-shape which first establishes brow-line and median-line in drawing or sculpting a portrait. Moreover, Vera's dance has created both 'ground' and 'figure'.

XIX Two graphic artists of Rilke's own time spring easily to the mind's eye. They are George Grosz for a picture of Money and her friends indulging in some light shopping, and Käthe Kollwitz for the blind beggar with his hand outstretched.

Gold, invisible, locked away 'somewhere' has become almost a concept of beauty through its utter abstractness: it is nearly but not quite equivalent to Money, which in turn stands for 'position' as much as for 'merchandise'. 'Gold is Capital, the most important thing in our "department-store-world" – yes, absolutely the living, pulsing, "breathing" part of it. Capitalism, together with Technology and Humanism, belongs to the [most] characterisitic manifestations of the *Zeit-Geist*' (Mörchen, 339). But perhaps 'Materialism' would be the more accurate diagnosis.

The Tenth Elegy's fairground scene has:

But something especially worth seeing is marked:
Adults only!
The Sex Life of Money. Full Anatomic Description.
Full Details.
More than a mere entertainment – how Money multiplies:
Its generative organs: Money in mating, at foreplay:
Instructive, amazing, arousing!

Elegies, 80, 81

In the Sonnet also, wealth is mocked in a relatively light-handed manner. 'Praise' is reserved for the everlastingly-outstretched hand of the blind beggar (something surely both moving and horrifying?). This hand, flexed, open, and as avid to receive as the wide-open anemone of Sonnet 2: V is also like the anemone kept open day and night.

There is a very long list of writings by Rilke in praise of the poor, the handicapped and the forgotten, of *Elend*, misery. Poverty, alienation and hardship are consistently seen (and perhaps sentimentalised) by him as offering a kind of nobility and freedom to those who must endure them. It is one of the tasks of Orpheus, God and Singer, to comprehend and to sing the riches of the destitute.

XX

> We have already had to rethink so many theories of planetary motion; in the same way we shall, little by little, learn to recognise that what we call destiny proceeds *from* humankind, is not introduced into us from outside. It was only because so many had not absorbed their destinies while they were still within them that they were unable to recognise what was proceeding from them – it seemed so alien that, in their confusion and alarm, they concluded that it must just now have entered them, for they would swear they had never before discovered anything like this in themselves. Just as we have for so long been mistaken about the progression of the sun, we continue to misunderstand the progression of what is to come. The future stands fast, my dear Herr Kappus, while we ourselves move through infinite Space.
>
> Br Kappus, 12 August 1904

'Ein Frühlingswind', a Rilke poem of 1907 written in Capri, discusses *Schicksal* in similar terms, as something intrinsic to us, a part of our own selves (SW II, 16).

The Fourth Elegy has:

> Who will show us what children really are?
> Who sets them in the constellations, puts
> a yardstick to tell *difference* in their hands?
>
> *Elegies*, 42, 43

The Sonnet's subject is 'destiny', but then all poetry, all art, all life, in one way or another has destiny as its subject. It is also about *Abstand*, 'difference' or 'disparity', and about 'discourse'.

For destiny, 'Fate' sounds more appropriate when 'she' is personified. When Fate is courting or being courted she does not make her intentions in the least apparent. What might serve to make intention or meaning clear is 'discourse', although Rilke is more than most aware both of the shortcomings of speech and of the profundities that can belong to silence. When discourse succeeds, a circle closes.

XXI Isfahan, renowned for its lavish irrigation systems and for the fertile soil of the region, and Shiraz, famous for its rose-gardens, are best known to Westerners for their carpets. The word *Teppich* occurs, resoundingly, at the conclusion of the Sonnet: the German word stands not only for 'carpet' but also for 'tapestry'.

Sonnet 2: XXI has been dated between 17 and 23 February. The Fifth Elegy, with its very different carpet, is dated 14 February (it was in fact the last of the Elegies to be written). The carpet of the Elegy is the 'tattered old mat' on which the impoverished Saltimbanques are obliged to perform – but it is in the end apotheosised as a magic carpet, on which the lovers stand and where they receive their 'coins of everlasting happiness'.

A Persian carpet is both a textile and a picture. Just as in a painting, in addition to objects and animal or plant figures, 'space' is described or implied – in pigment, or, as here, by means of coloured thread. In this way, almost literally, 'airs' are rendered and made visible.

The Sonnets 2: XVII and XXI are closely related and mutually enlightening. In both we are in the gardens of a kind of Eastern Paradise. The 'Consolation' of the earlier poem has flowered here into an exalted evocation of *amor fati*: the Sonnet amounts to a call-to-life of unmistakable sincerity. Here are to be found the praise, the jubilation, the *love* of life, which Rilke craved and of which, at the end, he found himself capable.

'You must never forget,' Rilke told Frau Wunderly-Volkart at a time at which he was very close to death, 'you must never forget: life is a thing of splendour!'

XXII Here Rilke is divided between 'praise' and *Kulturpessimismus*, his never-ending suspicion of the *Neu-Zeit* and of its technological and cultural change. The grudging 'Destiny' of the first line of the Sonnet seems to deny Rilke's *amor fati* of the previous poem, for all that the mission of Orpheus must be to praise Destiny in all of her moods.

The Sonnet abounds in images of generosity set against images of excess: 'much' is answered by 'too-much'. There are *über*-words present in each of the first three stanzas, and present-by-implication in the fourth (too high! too hasty! too noisy!).

Sonnet 2: XXII and a long passage in the Seventh Elegy reflect one another's content very exactly (it is the passage beginning *Nirgends, Geliebte, wird Welt sein, als innen*), and this relatedness holds good to the very end of the Elegy (*Elegies*, 58–63). The Elegy's power-station finds its counterpart in the flying-machine of the Sonnet; 'aspiration' is set against 'utility', permanence against speed, vertical against horizontal – between the two poems and within each of them.

The argument is still continuing and it must continue forever: cultural Roundheads embattled against Cavaliers, William Morris against Henry Ford, Norman Foster against Prince Charles. Does it in the end amount to no more than 'tradition', against 'change'?

The *doch nur wie gedacht* of the Sonnet's final line can be interpreted in at least three different ways. All of them seem apposite.

XXIII The Sonnet is, not so strangely, addressed by Rilke 'to the reader'. In it, Orpheus seems to offer to assist us, his readers, at our times of disappointment and frustration – which may, moreover, at the same time represent a kind of freedom from our expectations.

The First Elegy ends with the poet's citation of the Lament for Linos. According to one legend, Linos was a son of Apollo, and his death and mourning gave occasion to 'the first music'. Orpheus, too, and also according to only one of the many variant legends, is a son of Apollo. The conclusion of the Elegy reads:

> ...das Leere in jene
> Schwingung geriet, die uns jetzt hinreißt und tröstet and hilft.
> (Music: which 'ravishes, comforts and aids us'.)
>
> *Elegies*, 24, 25

Rilke's own cultural dilemma and the ups and downs of his *Kulturpessimismus* are neatly sketched-in at the third stanza, while the conclusion of the Sonnet bears the reminder that Mankind itself 'is' all those very dangers that we view with apprehension. (See again Sonnet 2: XX.)

XXIV The first stanza has landsmen putting aside their digging and, instead, putting out to sea. The 'loosened clay' makes their self-transplanting the easier. Self-reliant and fortunate, they are destined to drop anchor in some exquisite Mediterranean inlet where they will, little by little, construct their township (Positano? Lerici?).

Gods, according to Rilke in *this* Sonnet, are the work of human artist–artificers, while their provenance or suppression owes everything to the Master's mood.

A poem of 1906 by the temporarily disenchanted Rilke describes the magisterial Auguste Rodin, once the young poet's 'God', as the gaoler whose 'grubby eye' peers malevolently at him through his keyhole. Rodin may be personified here as *das mürrische Schicksal*, but if so he surely also doubles as one of the immortals, who must be heard and will hear 'at the end'. The poem, 'Der Gefangene', appears in *Neue Gedichte* Part I (NG, 58–61).

The infant whom we, unwisely, await with such enthusiasm may turn out to be a young Frankenstein-monster: the infant-technology.

The last stanza connects with the first in its praise of Man the Explorer, leased out by Death to his own profit and to the great advantage of World.

XXV Rilke, not always an enthusiast for understatement, once described the colouring of 'Chicken, Herring and Apple' as more nearly resembling 'Parrot, Goldfish and Orange' when painted by Otto Modersohn (Mörchen, 482, n. 21). This *Vorfrühlingsonnet* has fierce saturated blacks and some faint tints, but it contains practically no colour at all and is in a sense understated, *enthalten*.

The Part 2 Sonnet is described by Rilke himself as the companion-piece to 'the little Spring-Song', that is to Sonnet 1: XXI. The high key and the white snows of the winter schoolroom are replaced by the black, brooding stillness of all that is, here, still waiting to occur. The latent energy of the Sonnet is remarkable; its feeling of powers still reined-in. But, does it truly belong to the cycle at all?

At first sight Sonnets 2: XXIV and XXV seem of an entirely different mood: nevertheless, they are related. Both Sonnets commence with an image of Mankind engaged in tilling Earth's soil, the very clay of which Man himself was created. Both Sonnets are 'pregnant', both focused firmly on 'future', on *Zukunft*, in the one instance represented by an infant (or a portent?), in the other by a season (an infant season). So much for similarities. What of the differences?

Sonnet 2: XXIV seems to paint a picture of *southern* temperateness and sweetness. There is oil in the jars, not butter or lard, and although wine is not specified it is, surely, implied. The present Sonnet, on the other hand, is hauntingly similar in mood to 'Die Insel, Nordsee' of the *Neue Gedichte*, an uncompromisingly northern piece of land-and-sea-scape which was perhaps derived from Rilke's experience of the landscapes of North Germany in general: Worpswede, Westerwede, Oberneuland (NG, 112–17). In their quite different ways the landscapes of both Sonnets are beautiful: one sweet, the other acid.

Where and when Sonnet 2: XXV was written is not in doubt: it is dated 19–23 February and its provenance is, of course, Muzot. Furthermore, a verse fragment of the same date has been preserved which reads:

Von meiner Antwort weiß ich noch nicht
wann ich sie sagen werde.
Aber, horch eine Harke, die schon schafft.
Oben allein im Weinberg spricht
schon ein Mann mit der Erde.

SW II, 473–4

Rilke's opening : *Schon, horch, hörst du der ersten Harken / Arbeit;* should be read as the four-times-repeated imperative to 'Listen!'. The following Sonnet, too, will offer a new sound.

XXVI

...And already today I hear the children less loudly. There are hordes of them and they make a terrible din in the Campo San Vio. I would never have believed that any ears could have the sheer capacity to take it all in; they carry on with the persistence of dangerous lunatics – but I am no longer upset, I shall get used to it, there is no point in dwelling on details – and taken as a whole it adds up to a kind of exaggerated silence! In the end one might come to hear the whole thing as we hear the many flocks of sparrows, who give voice to something halfway between the joyfulness and the malice of life: it is hard to be sure which!

Br Taxis I, 163

The hyperaesthetic Rilke was inevitably also *lärmempfindlich*, sensitive to noise. Children and wildlife might be thought to have something in common, but the Eighth Elegy, too, proposes that human self-awareness distorts the natural predispositions of even the youngest children, rendering them somehow wrong-hearted in relation to the *Weltall*.

Mörchen suggests that the *Sonnets* reach their lowest point in this poem; lowest, that is in terms of Rilke's own pessimism. It is also suggested that this is an 'Autumn Sonnet'; that the winds buffeting the kites of the children must be the winds of autumn (Mörchen, 390, 384).

Rodin spoke with bitterness of 'this cruel joke to which they give the name of Cubism'. It may be that 2: XXVI is the Sonnet of Rilke's own deepest *Kulturpessimismus*, not in relation to the technology but to the *art* of his own times and that, thoroughly hostile to many of the radical artistic manifestations of the era, Rilke is raising his own loud cry of protest.

In the visual arts, German Expressionism had succeeded in welding together aspects of tribal art on the one hand and European painting at its most advanced on the other. In those years a woodcarving by Kirchner, of distinctly 'ethnic' appearance, might have been found in a reinforced-concrete apartment together with modernistic furniture (and still, perhaps, a copy of the *Cornet*).

The Fifth Elegy, written entirely around Picasso's *Les Saltimbanques* of 1905, is dated 14 February 1922: in it Rilke has steeped himself in his memory of a picture painted seventeen years before. *Les Demoiselles d'Avignon*, completed in 1909, a painting vociferous with *Neu-Zeit*, seems likely on the other hand to have been for Rilke only one more milestone on the road of his cultural alienation.

The screaming children fill the poet with irritation and alarm. They are far from the as-yet-uncorrupted, the unenfranchised waifs towards whom he normally demonstrates such sympathy: these are miniature Yahoos; little Maenads! Here is only dissonance and lawlessness, unshaped and un-evolved, a crying that seeks to rely on expression alone. The Sonnet recalls the earlier description of Grief attempting, 'inaccurate and artless', to raise the voice of humankind to the high heavens (Sonnet 1: VIII). The whole text requires little interpretation to be read as Rilke's statement that Orpheus represents – as well as lyric freedom – a certain order and restraint. No kite can fly without its string. (See also Letter to N.N., 26 December 1911: Br I, 322–3.)

XXVII Time is entropy. As in Sonnet 1: XII, the ticking footsteps of clocks pursue Mankind through the garden, in the house, in the street, in the trenches. 'Time' is also 'Death'; complete with hourglass and scythe, the tools of his trade. What might resist him?

Ach, das Gespenst des Vergänglichen, introduces counter-arguments to Rilke's praise of the little anemone in its unremitting 'taking-in'. His text may be self-admonishment, for the very long years between 1914 and 1922 were also very lean in achievement.

Who cheats the pawky Fates
By what he does, not is,
By what he makes, imposing
On flux an architectonic –

Louis MacNeice, *Plant and Phantom*

In Sonnet 1: XXII Rilke seemed to look askance at Mankind in its 'striving', whereas the present Sonnet claims that it is in action alone that Man and the Immortals regularly touch fingers. Even Death 'knows how greatly he profits in leasing us out' (Sonnet 2: XXIV).

XXVIII The Sonnet is a second requiem for Vera, whose citadel has in the end been stormed by Time and Death. Nevertheless the first stanza apostrophises her in the present tense as if the Singing God had once more brought a latter-day Eurydice back, for a while, from the Shades.

The dancer's 'coming and going' repeat the comings and goings of Orpheus himself in all his *Metamorphosen* in Sonnet 1: V, and they are moreover not only the movements of this dance but also of The Dance – a birth, a life, a death.

Art exceeds Nature, says the Sonnet, and Nature stands in need of Art to reach her own most richly-sentient potentials.

In the sestet it is by means of *memory* that the part-childish, part-divine spirit of Vera–Eurydice has become custodian of an arcane and sacred treasure: of the tradition of the genesis and first vibrations of the Song of Orpheus (see again the first of the *Elegies*).

The Song is not for the Singer. It is not for any who may listen. The Song is for itself.

XXIX It is addressed: 'To a friend of Vera' and is clearly Rilke addressing Rilke. From it can be inferred that many of the previous

Sonnets' admonitions and injunctions are also self-addressed. When, as he so often does, Rilke writes *du*, is he speaking to himself or to his reader? And, does the answer to the question really matter? For the writer is invariably his own first reader and is appropriately metamorphosed by the change of role.

The tone of invocation of this Sonnet is in a subtle manner a different voice from any of the other *Sonnets to Orpheus*, a tone that seems, almost to a hairsbreadth, half-way between that of the *Neue Gedichte* and that of the *Elegies*: it would be tempting to relate the imperatives to the *Elegies* and the images to the *Neue Gedichte*; tempting, but little more than half-true.

Stiller Freund der vielen Fernen may mean either 'distant places' or 'distant people'. However the whole first stanza of the Sonnet carries an echo of the final lines of 'Der Einsame' from the *Neue Gedichte*: *das die Weiten, die es still vernichten / zwingen, immer seliger zu sein.* ('While silently the distances destroy / what they compel to ever greater joy.' NG, 266, 267.)

Stille, *Ferne*, *Raum* are very much the kind of currency to which Rilke returns again and again with reliable fidelity.

Each stanza of the Sonnet in German carries a pair of imperatives, although in the first triplet the commands have been run together. The first stanza of the poem recalls not only 'Der Einsame' but also 'Der Turm' of the *Neue Gedichte* (NG, 102, 103). More locally, it picks up the theme of *Atmen, du unsichtbares Gedicht* from the initial Sonnet of Part 2.

The second stanza uses *Verwandlung* to point back briefly towards the 'Seek transformation' theme of Sonnet 2: XII. There may also be an even slighter reference intended to the 'bitter beer' of the Tenth Elegy's fairground (the entire fairground scene is a kind of sociological *Neu-Zeit*-study: there is nothing in the *Sonnets* that resembles it at all).

Kreuzweg makes the connection with Sonnet 1: III and its crossroad, at which no temple of Apollo can be built. The word *Übermaß*, 'excess', signals that here too any 'magic' can have nothing at all to do with the clear-eyed God of Measure. The final stanza of this final Sonnet is what it must be: a kind of farewell. It has an appropriately biblical, perhaps even a faintly rabbinical tone: In a storm, stand! In a calm, sail!

'Earth' also means 'soil': the double antithesis sets flow against stasis, liquid against solid, *wandeln* against *bleiben*.

LETTERS TO A YOUNG POET

Introduction

Why do budding authors write to famous seniors enclosing examples of their work? You can ask this question cynically and come up with the expectedly cynical answer. They wish to hear that they have some gift and, in practical terms, that their distinguished mentor will help launch them on their chosen career (or perhaps one might say, the career they have chosen as appropriate to their idea of themselves). Sometimes the process works in just this worldly way. Usually it doesn't. But even if one is to take the cynical view there is something true in such an impulse. What we all want when we start out is a signal, a recognition by an established creator that we have the call, that one day we may be permitted to join the professionals, the party of the elect. Writers especially, poets perhaps most of all, are driven by a terrible technical uncertainty. The Medieval and Renaissance tradition of an apprenticeship, of joining a master's workshop or atelier has not died out even today among musicians, painters and sculptors. But it was never so strong among writers, other than in a limited sense among theologians, and now it is almost extinct (or was until the Americans introduced the Creative Writing School). In the Romantic era the very name of poet suggested a sort of doomed individual filled with alienation. Thus, straining to satisfy the doubt which was an integral part of his adopted passion, the young poet sought a master, not as an apprentice would enter a workshop, but as a spiritual pilgrim might attach himself to some illuminatus or a mystic to a guru.

The real test of an aspirant writer's seriousness was and is the master he or she chooses as desired mentor. If it's a great professor, a boulevard playwright or best-selling novelist, then 'career' is likely to be the prime mover. Poets, however, frequently pick an eccentric reputation, one more notorious than celebrated. There is a tradition among poets that they see themselves, however much this may be a mask to their uncertainty, as rebels, resisters of established modes, and so they choose controversial figures to sit at the feet of. Poetry more than the other literary arts practises a form of apostolic succession. There are a few paradoxes attached to this, however – some highly original artists prefer to learn from conservative practitioners. When the young Rimbaud announced from Charleville that he would soon come to Paris, he did not write to Verlaine but to Théodore de Banville, indicating his intention of joining the company of the Parnassians. Similarly, the revolutionary Stravinsky had the traditionalist Rimsky-Korsakov as teacher; on the other hand Arnold Schönberg received the baton of experiment from Gustav Mahler and Samuel Beckett took over from James Joyce. The one thing which is certain is that the act of identifying an older and reputed mentor is always an egotistical one. The hope is to partake of some sort of suction: virtue will drain out of the elder into the younger figure.

When the naïve but oddly attractive young military cadet Franz Xaver Kappus first wrote to Rainer Maria Rilke in 1902, he was without doubt aware of his model's unorthodoxy in the world of German poetry. From the moment of Rilke's answering his first letter until Kappus's announcement of his acceptance of a non-poetic career, which brought the correspondence to an end in 1908, Kappus received ten letters of outstanding admonishment and encouragement. Kappus had a personal reason for approaching Rilke and not some other German master: Rilke, too, had found himself alienated from the ambience of a military academy when a couple of decades previously he had been a cadet, first at St Pölten and later at Mährisch-Weisskirchen. It is questionable whether Rilke's advice helped Kappus make up his mind about the conflict of loyalties between his desire to be a poet and his need to make a successful career in some more worldly profession. From the start Rilke's letters were almost impossibly high-minded and must have been received by Kappus with mixed feelings. To his credit, Kappus appreciated how remarkable the advice he was getting was, and how beautifully it was expressed. Like so many published exchanges of letters, this one attains an artificial detachment by the total suppression of one side of the correspondence. There is a remarkable moment when Rilke observes that he has written out one of Kappus's sonnets in his own hand and is enclosing it with his reply. Only a transcendent egoist would do such a thing. There is not a shred of practical criticism of Kappus's poetry in the whole body of Rilke's letters, though there is much remarkable discussion of literature in general terms. Rilke the alchemist stands clearly in view. It is almost as if his copying out of Kappus's poem could turn the young man's uninspired effort from base metal to true gold.

Rilke died unexpectedly in 1926. He had for many years been German Literature's most celebrated living poet, but also its most uneasy adornment. He was neither a Modernist nor a Traditionalist. He remained a Rilkeist all his life. In 1929 Kappus remembered those letters of twenty-five years before, saw how potent they were, and decided to print them for the greater glory of German Art. In this he was right, though the fact that it was as an aspirant poet he first wrote to Rilke gives the sequence a misleading emphasis. Rilke writes as a great and original moral teacher – admittedly one in whom morality is inseparable from the highest concern for literature. But *Letters to a Young Idealist* might be a better title. Rilke probably received many manuscripts from hopeful authors. When Kappus wrote, something in his epistolary manner or perhaps in the poems he sent aroused in Rilke a desire for *ex cathedra* pronouncement. His replies to Kappus are impersonal, however impassioned – only occasionally does he illustrate his arguments with accounts of his own sufferings.

Many of Rilke's perceptions are ahead of their time, and much of his comment on literature is profound. He warns against literary criticism and journalism: 'stay away from every genre that is familiar or obvious', he advises. A more direct warning concerns irony, though there Rilke also reminds Kappus that irony imaginatively used is a proper tool of the poet. It is no use seeking answers to problems in the abstract, Rilke tells him, you must find answers you can *live*. Rilke's approach to sexuality (clearly the young Kappus's *croce delizia*) is imaginative and innovative. One letter finds Rilke anticipating his rival Hofmansthal's hymn to human fertility in *Die Frau ohne Schatten*. Human life is the bridge over which the great dead pass to their new life. Rilke also forecasts that women will soon be seen to outpace men in feeling and understanding. He links up with Freud in the belief that human beings have the power to heal themselves through deep analysis of their inward experience. He has a healthy distrust of our century's passion for categorising: the very name of a transgression may help wreck a life, he declares.

All this is expressed in very beautiful prose. For English readers it is as if Henry James were reborn in a psychologically-inclined Teutonic writer. That we can read these letters as if they were from James or Keats is a tribute to Stephen Cohn's supremely natural translation. Rilke has always been dear to English speakers, however improbable or unwelcome such an affection might have seemed to him. This short collection shows an unexpectedly generous side to his talent. It should be read with Rilke's poetry in mind.

PETER PORTER

Preface

It was late autumn in the year 1902 and I was sitting beneath ancient chestnut trees in the park of the Military Academy in Wiener-Neustadt, reading a book. I was so deep in my reading that I scarcely noticed that someone had sat down to join me: it was the Academy's chaplain, the learned and good-natured Professor Horaček, the only one of our instructors who was not an army officer. He plucked the book from my hand, looked at its cover and shook his head: 'Poems by Rainer Maria Rilke?' he mused. He leafed through its pages, glanced at one or two poems, gazed thoughtfully into the distance and finally nodded. 'So it seems that our pupil René Rilke became a poet.'

He told me of a slight, pale-faced youngster, sent by his parents to the Junior Military School in St Pölten more than fifteen years before, so that he might eventually become an officer. Horaček had been the institution's chaplain at the time. He recalled his former pupil perfectly and described him as a quiet, serious boy who preferred to keep himself apart but had patiently put up with the restrictions of his life as a boarder. After completing his fourth year he graduated with the others to the Senior Military School in Mährisch-Weisskirchen. There it became evident that his constitution was not in fact robust enough for such a life, so that in the end his parents took him home and arranged for him to continue his education in Prague. Horaček knew nothing of his subsequent career and could tell me no more.

Given all this, it is easy to understand why I then and there resolved that I would send my own attempts at poetry to Rainer Maria Rilke and ask him to give me his opinion of them. Less than twenty years old, on the threshold of a career which I sensed was completely contrary to all my inclinations, I believed I might find understanding from the author of *Mir zur Feier* if I was to find it anywhere at all. Almost without my volition a letter was composed to accompany my poems, and in it I bared my soul more unreservedly than I ever had before, and more than I would ever again reveal it to another.

Many weeks went by before the reply came. The letter with its blue sealing-wax felt heavy in my hand. It was postmarked Paris and its envelope was addressed in the clear, fine, bold calligraphy that characterised its contents throughout. This was the beginning of my regular exchange of letters with Rainer Maria Rilke which was to continue steadily until 1908 – but then it gradually petered out, for my own life had led me into just those circumstances from which Rilke's warm and kind concern had sought to protect me.

But that is unimportant. It is the ten letters that follow that are important, for it is important that they should become known in the world in which Rainer Maria Rilke lived and achieved his work; furthermore they are important for those who are still growing and becoming, today and tomorrow. And when one who is great and unique speaks to us, it is for lesser men to fall silent.

Berlin, June 1929 FRANZ XAVER KAPPUS

I

Paris, 17 February 1903

My dear Sir,
Your letter did not reach me until a few days ago: I thank you for its trustingness and for its great good faith. I cannot do much more than that. I am really not able to discuss the nature of your poems, for I am much too far from having any ambitions as a critic: there is nothing which touches works of art so little as does the language of criticism: nothing ever comes of that but more or less felicitous misunderstandings. Few things are in fact as accessible to reason or to language as people will generally try to make us believe. Most phenomena are *unsayable*, and have their being in a dimension which no word has ever entered; and works of art are the most unsayable of all – they are mysterious presences whose lives endure alongside our own perishable lives.

Having made this declaration in advance, I can only tell you that your poems have nothing that is quite particular to them, but that quietly and secretly they are beginning to tend toward something more personal. I can sense this most clearly in the last of the poems, 'Meine Seele'. There is something original in it trying to be felt, to be heard. And in the beautiful poem 'An Leopardi' there is perhaps a growing kinship with that great and solitary man. All the same, the poems are not yet things in their own right, independent entities. The letter which you kindly sent me with them does, it is true, explain a number of shortcomings which I sensed while I was reading the poems, even though I could not identify and name them.

You ask if your poems are good poems. You are asking me, but you will surely have asked others before me. You doubtless send your poems out to the magazines and you are distressed each time the editors reject your efforts. You have permitted me to offer you advice, and my advice is that you should give all that up. You are looking outwards and that, above all, is what you should not be doing at this time. There is no-one who can advise or who can aid you; no-one. There is only one way. *You must go inside yourself.* You must seek for whatever it is that obliges you to write. You must discover if its roots reach down to the very depths of your heart. You must confess to yourself whether you would truly die if writing were forbidden to you. This above all: ask yourself in the night, in your most silent hour – *Must* I write? If there is an affirmative reply, if you can simply and starkly answer '*I must*' to that grave question, then you will need to construct your life according to that necessity. Even in its most trivial and commonplace moments your life must be the expression of and the witness to that imperative. And then you must approach the world of Nature. Like primeval man, you must try to tell of what you see and experience and love and have lost. Do not try to write love-poems. To begin with you should stay away from every genre that is familiar or obvious, for those are the most difficult to master. You will require a great deal of talent and maturity before you can contribute anything of your own to a tradition that has, already, so many good and sometimes brilliant exemplars. Consequently you should avoid the commoner subjects of poetry and favour the subjects which your own day-to-day experience can offer you: depict your sorrows and your hopes; your ever-changing preoccupations; your faith in some kind of beauty; depict it all with quiet, humble, passionate sincerity and use the things all around you to express it: the images of your dreams, the objects you keep in your memory. If your daily life seems mean to you – do not find fault with it; rather chide yourself that you are not poet enough to evoke its riches: if one is truly creative there is no such thing as poverty, and no place that is poor or meaningless. Even if you were kept in a prison whose walls permitted no sound to reach your senses from the outside world – would you not still possess your childhood, that marvellous realm, that treasure-house of recollections? Direct your attention towards *that*. Try to salvage your own feelings, to draw them up from those depths of long-ago: your sense of yourself will grow stronger and your solitariness will open and will become a twilight place of habitation in which the sounds that other people make are faint and far away. And if poems should be born of this inwardness, this immersion in a private world, it will not even occur to you to ask anyone if they are 'good'; nor will you try to interest the periodicals in these works of yours. You will see in them your own precious and appropriate inheritance, a piece of your own life which speaks with your own voice.

A work of art is 'good' only if it came into being out of some necessity. It is in this way and in no other that it can be judged. And that, my dear Sir, is why I can do no more than give you this advice: to enter right inside yourself and to examine the origins of your own life; that is the source at which you will find out whether or not you are called upon to be a Maker. Whatever answer comes, take it. Do not interpret it. It may emerge that you are called upon to be an artist. If so, you must accept that destiny and you must bear it, enduring both its burden and its greatness, and not expect any recompense from the world outside you. The creative man must be his own world and must find all he needs within himself, and in the natural world of which he has made himself a part.

But it may be that you will have to decide against becoming a poet, even when you have made that descent deep down into your self. As I have already said, it is enough to feel that one *could* survive without writing for one to be actually proscribed from doing so. And all the same this descent that I ask of you would still not have been wasted; for after it your life will be sure to find the ways that are its own, and I wish you, more than I can say, that they may be good, fruitful and generous.

What more should I say to you? It seems to me that things come to pass as they are meant to. In the end I really only want to counsel you to stay patient and wise while you are still developing your self; nothing could be more harmful for you than to look outwards and seek, outside yourself, answers to the questions which only your own deepest instincts, in their own quietest moments, might perhaps be able to answer.

I was delighted to come across Professor Horaček's name in your letter; I retain a deep respect for that amiable scholar and my gratitude to him has not lessened over the years. Please be good enough to tell him so; it is kind of him still to remember me, and I do appreciate it.

I return herewith the poems which you kindly entrusted to me, and I thank you once again for the candour and good faith with which you did so. Although we are strangers to one another I have tried to deserve your trust by sending you this honestly-given reply, the best that I could find to give you.

With my sincere good wishes

Rainer Maria Rilke

II

Viareggio near Pisa (Italy), 5 April 1903

You must forgive me, my dear Sir, for not replying to your letter until today: I have all the time been not exactly ill but afflicted with an influenza-like weariness which has made me incapable of anything. In the end, as nothing else would do, I made my way down to this southern coast whose virtues have restored me once before. But I am still not really well. I find writing difficult, so you must take these few lines in token of more.

You should know that, of course, each one of your letters will always bring me pleasure, but you must be tolerant towards my replies for they may often leave you with nothing in your hands: in the end it is in the most fundamental and crucial of our concerns that we remain unutterably alone. A great deal has to take place for one person to be able to advise or, even more, actually to aid another; a whole constellation of things must come together for that to be successful even once.

Today there are only two things that I want to say to you.

Irony: do not let yourself be governed by it, especially in your everyday concerns. In your creative work try to make use of it as one more means of catching hold of life. Used purely, irony itself is pure and you need not be ashamed of making use of it. If you feel that you rely on it too often, if you fear that you may come to rely on it more and more, turn your attention towards the great and serious subjects before which irony stands helpless and diminished. Seek out the depths of things: irony will not penetrate so deep; and if this brings you right up to the margins of great matters, then ask yourself if an ironic interpretation is born of some inner need of your own nature. Under the influence of serious subjects, irony will leave you alone if it is merely something fortuitous. But if it is something fundamental to you, a part of your own birthright, it will grow to become a useful tool and it will find an orderly place among the things by means of which you will construct your art.

Here is the second thing that I wanted to tell you today:

Among all my books there are only a few that I cannot be without. But there are two which I take with me everywhere, wherever I may be. I have them with me now. They are the Bible and the works of the great Danish poet Jens Peter Jacobsen. I wonder if you know his works? You can easily acquire them, for some have been brought out by Reclam's Universal Library in a very good translation. Get yourself the little volume *Six Stories*, by J.P. Jacobsen, and his novel *Neils Lyhne*; you should start with the first novella of the first volume, entitled *Mogens*. A world will open up around you; the fortune, the treasures and the greatness of an entire world. You should live for a while in these books and learn from them whatever seems to you worth learning. But first and foremost learn to love them. They will repay your love a thousand times over and, whatever paths your own life may take, I am certain that these books will remain among the most important threads in the fabric of your living, of all your happenings and of your joys and disappointments.

If I had to say from whom I had learned to experience something of the nature of the creative act, of its profundity and of its enduringness, I could cite only two names: that of Jacobsen, that truly great poet; and that of Auguste Rodin the sculptor, who has no equal among the artists of our time.

I wish you success in everything!

Yours

Rainer Maria Rilke

III

Viareggio near Pisa (Italy), 23 April 1903

Your Easter letter, my dear Sir, gave me a great deal of pleasure, for it told me so many good things about you. The manner in which you wrote about Jacobsen's great and tender artistry showed me that I did right in trying to guide your life and its many questions towards that generous abundance.

Now you must discover *Neils Lyhne*, that book of splendours and profundities. The more you read it the more it seems to encompass everything there is, from life's faintest fragrances to the full, pungent flavour of its weightiest fruit. The book contains nothing that has not been comprehended, grasped, undergone and understood in the re-echoing and vibrant aftersounds of memory; no experience is too circumscribed for it and the smallest happening unfolds as if it were destiny; while destiny itself is like a wonderful white tapestry, its threads placed next to one another by an infinitely scrupulous hand – to be finally lifted up and carried by a hundred hands. You will experience the great good fortune of reading the book for the first time, meeting its countless surprises as if you were living in a new dream. But I can promise you that you will ever live in these books with the same sense of astonishment, and that you will lose none of their marvellous power, none of the legendary quality which overcomes you on first reading them.

In reading them one grows ever more responsive, ever more grateful, somehow better and simpler in one's vision, deeper in one's convictions, stronger and more joyful in living.

And later you must read *Marie Grubbe*, that marvellous story of destiny and yearning, and Jacobsen's letters, and pages from his diaries, and various fragments and, finally, his poems which (although the translation is no more than mediocre) have a tone that will resound forever. (Furthermore, I suggest that if you can you should buy the handsome complete edition of Jacobsen's works, which includes all this. It is published in three volumes, in a good translation, by Eugen Diederichs of Leipzig, and it costs, so I believe, only five or six marks for each volume.)

Of course you are absolutely and incontestably right in your judgement of *Hier sollten Rosen stehen*...(a work of matchless subtlety and wonderfully formed), in contrast to the views of the author of the Introduction. And let me straight away make this plea to you: endeavour to read as little aesthetic criticism as possible. Things of that sort are either received opinions, opinions grown petrified and meaningless, insensitive and far-removed from anything alive; or else they are clever word-games in which one view may prevail today and the converse view tomorrow. Works of art are infinitely solitary, and nothing comes so little near them as does criticism. It is love alone that can grasp them and hold them and can do them justice. You should always trust yourself and your own intuitions against that kind of analysis or argument or presentation. And if you should make mistakes, then the natural growth of your own inner life will little by little and in due time guide you towards different insights. You must permit your own judgement to develop quietly and undisturbed; like all true progress, that will originate from deep within you and cannot be forced or hastened. To carry, come to term, give birth, is *everything*. To allow each thing its own evolution, each impression and each grain of feeling buried in the self, in the darkness, unsayable, unknowable, and with infinite humility and patience to await the birth of a new illumination: this alone is what it means to live the life of an artist – in understanding as much as in creating.

Here there can be no measurement by time; a year does not signify and even a decade means nothing. To be an artist means that you cannot enumerate or calculate but must grow as the trees grow – letting the sap flow at its own pace, standing firm through the gales of spring, never fearing lest there should be no summer. For there *will* be summer. But only for those who stay as patient as if all eternity lay before them, expansive, steady, unperturbed. I have to learn this lesson every day anew and learn it painfully, and am thankful for the pain: *patience* is everything!

Richard Dehmel: something about his books (and incidentally about the man too, although I do not know him well) makes me feel that whenever I have come to one of his best pages I must be fearful of the next – for it may tear everything to shreds again and transform what was admirable into something unworthy. Your phrase 'living and writing by sensuality' sums him up quite well. And truly the experience of the artist is so unbelievably close to the sexual, both in its pain and in its pleasure, that they are really only different manifestations of the same longing and of the same fulfilment. And if it were possible to say 'sexual' instead of 'sensual' – 'sexual' in its largest and purest and most generous meaning, and not traduced by any church nonsense – then his artistry would be very great indeed and of infinite significance. For he has great force as a poet, strong as a primal urge; it carries its own reckless rhythms with it and it bursts out from him like a mountain torrent.

And yet it is as if that power were not always absolutely genuine and free from affectation. (Though that is indeed one of the severest tests by which an artist can be judged – that he must ever remain innocent and unaware of his greatest powers, if he is not to rob them of their freedom, of their purity.) Consequently, when this force of his comes rushing through his being and reaches its sexual focus, it encounters there a human creature who is by no means as pure as it had needed him to be. Instead of a pure and fully ripened sexuality it encounters one that is not *human* enough but merely *masculine*, merely lustful and drunken and restless and laden with all the old prejudice and arrogance with which men have persecuted and disfigured love. It is because he loves *only* as a male and never as a human creature that his perception of sexuality so often contains something mean, and seems savage, malicious, provisional, circumscribed, and this diminishes his art and leaves it ambiguous and somehow dubious. It is far from immaculate, it is shaped by the age and by passion, and little of it will prevail and endure. (And yet, this is true of most art!) And in spite of all this one may truly rejoice at what is great in his work, although one must take pains not to become lost in it, not to become indentured to that Dehmel-world, so infinitely fearful, so full of madness and adultery; and so far from our own true destinies which, though they involve more suffering than these provisional sadnesses, offer a better chance of greatness and more courage to face eternity.

Finally, as regards my own books: I would be more than happy to send you every one of them that might conceivably interest you. However, I am extremely poor and my books once published are no longer mine. I cannot afford to buy them myself, as I would like to, and to send them to the people who would cherish them.

And so I will note down for you a list of the titles (and the publishers) of the most recently published (only the recentest, for I must have published twelve or thirteen altogether). I shall have to leave it to you, my dear Sir, to order some of them, as and when you can.

I am happy to think of my books in your possession.

I wish you well.

Yours

Rainer Maria Rilke

IV

At Worpswede bei Bremen, 16 July 1903

About ten days ago, thoroughly sick and weary, I left Paris and made my way to this great northern plain: its vastness, its stillness and its skies are to nurse me back to health again. But I journeyed right into solid rain; today for the first time the skies are trying to brighten and I am taking advantage of these first moments of light to send you, my dear Sir, a greeting.

My dear Herr Kappus, I have left a letter of yours unanswered for a long time. It is not that I had forgotten it; on the contrary, it was the kind of letter anyone would read a second time if he chanced on it again among his papers, and I could recognise you in it as if you were standing beside me. It was your letter of the second of May. I am sure you remember it. Reading it as I do now, in the great stillness of this faraway place, I am touched by your wonderful concern for life even more than I was in Paris, for there everything sounds different, smothered by the inordinate din that agitates everything. Here, in the midst of this enormous landscape and of the great winds that blow across it from the sea, I feel that there is no-one who could find answers to those questions of yours, those emotions, which deep within themselves live a life of their own. Even the best of us cannot quite find words that will truly express things so subtle and virtually unsayable. Nevertheless I believe that you need not stay unanswered so long as you keep in touch with things resembling those by which my eyes are at this moment refreshed. If you keep close to Nature, to all that is simple in Nature, to the small things which scarcely anyone notices and which can for that very reason invisibly lead to what is great, what is immeasurable; if you truly possess this love for lesser things and if, by serving them, you can quietly win the trust of things that seem humble – then everything will grow easier for you, more unified, somehow more reconciling, not necessarily in your *mind*, which may hesitate, amazed, but in your deepest awareness and watchfulness and understanding. You are still so young, so uncommitted, and I do entreat you as strongly as I can, my dear Sir, to stay patient with all that is still unresolved in your own heart, to try to love the very *questions*, just as if they were locked-up rooms or as if they were books in an utterly unknown language. You ought not yet to be searching for answers, for you could not yet *live* them. What matters is to live everything. For just now, live the questions. Maybe you will little by little, almost without noticing, one distant day live your way into the answers. It may be that you do possess inside you the potential to create images and forms, as a way of living that is especially joyous and direct. Educate yourself for it – but accept whatever comes your way and trust it unreservedly: even if it seems no more than *willed*, out of some inner need of your own, take it to yourself and do not despise it. Sex is no easy subject, it is true, but it is the hard subjects that we were set and there is little of importance that is not onerous. If only you can accept that and, from your own nature and predisposition, from *your* experiences, from out of *your* own childhood and out of the strength that is *yours*, win an attitude towards sex that (freed from custom and convention) is truly your own…then you no longer need be afraid that you might lose yourself, that you might grow unworthy of your most valuable possession.

Sexual pleasure is one experience of our senses, not so far different from seeing or from the pure sensation of tasting a delicious fruit; it is a great never-ending experience, a thing that we are given, a means of knowing our world, our brightest, our most lavish means of knowing it. It is by no means bad that we should embrace it. What is bad is that most of us squander and misuse this experience, that we make use of it to stimulate the weary parts of our lives, that we use it for a diversion and not as a call for us to scale the heights! Mankind has even transformed *eating* into something that it never was. On the one hand deprivation and on the other excess have spoiled the directness of our appetite, and all the deepest, most straightforward basic drives by means of which life renews itself have been spoiled in the same manner. And yet the *individual* can still cleanse them for himself and can live purely (not, perhaps, the *single* individual, who may remain dependent, but the *solitary*). For he will not forget that all the beauty of animals and plants is nothing but a lasting manifestation of love, of longing; he can watch animals and plants alike, patient and content to mate and to reproduce and to grow, not driven by physical lust nor by physical need, but embracing necessities immeasurably greater than pleasure or pain, and more powerful than attraction or aversion. If only Mankind could accept this mystery which fills our world right down to its smallest creatures, if only he would experience it more humbly and more profoundly, recognising how terribly important it is instead of treating it so lightly. If only he could grow more reverent towards his fruitfulness – which is the same whether it is made manifest as flesh or as spirit: the creativity of the intellect and spirit originates in the physical, is of the same nature, and is a quieter and more lasting equivalent of sexual love. 'The impulse to create, to beget, to give form' counts for nothing without its powerful and lasting confirmation, its realisation in the world, and it is nothing without the assent of a host of objects and creatures: the experiencing of it is so wonderfully beautiful and so rewarding because it is charged with a heritage of memories – of the begetting and bearing of millions. A thousand nights of love are present and alive in every creative impulse and they exalt and ennoble it. Those who cling together by night, encradled and entwined in desire, perform an essential task: they gather sweetness, resonance and strength for the songs of some poet of the future who will rise up and who will speak the rapture that cannot be spoken. And furthermore they conjure up the future. And even if they cling blindly and in error to one another...the future is summoned nevertheless and a new creature rises up; and of the seemingly fortuitous event which takes place here is born the law by which one vigorous and resolute sperm must struggle towards the egg-cell drifting aspiringly towards it. Do not allow yourself to be misled by surfaces; it is in the depths that all is decided. Those who live this mystery poorly and falsely (and they are many) only forfeit it for themselves – and they transmit it nonetheless, like a sealed letter, without even knowing that they do so. See that the multiplicity of its names does not mislead you, nor its variety of instances. It may be that there is one maternity that governs everything, and that all things share in a common longing. The loveliness of maidens, of creatures 'who have not yet borne fruit' (as you so well put it), is the beauty of a motherhood in anticipation and in preparation – living both in hope and in fear. A mother's beauty is motherhood in function. In an old woman, it is a potent remembrance. And I believe that the principle of motherhood is to be found in the male as well, corporeally as well as abstractly, for the act of begetting is a kind of giving birth and, surely, man also gives birth to whatever things he may create out of his inner riches. It may be that the sexes are far closer related than is generally believed and that the great renewal of our world will be when young men and women, freed of all sense of sin and all uneasiness, instead of seeking for their opposites will join together like brother and sister, like good neighbours, as *human beings* in fact, so that they may help one another bear, carefully and patiently, the heavy sexuality that has been laid upon them.

But one who is alone can *already* build and prepare, with his own hands and with fewer mistakes, all that the many may one day be able to achieve. And so, my dear Sir, love your solitariness and bear the pain it gives you, and make of it a melody of lamentation. For the people near to you are far away, you tell me, and that signifies a widening of the space around you. And if what is close to you is distant, it means that your own distance reaches out beneath the stars and is very great: you should be glad that you are growing, although you can take no-one along with you; and you must stay kind to the people you leave behind, steady and gentle with them, neither tormenting them with your doubts nor frightening them with your certainties, with your joyfulness which they would not understand. Try to reach an easy and sincere relationship with them, and it can stay constant even if you yourself change more and more. Learn to love the life in them, so different from your own life. Be considerate of the people who are growing old, for they fear the solitariness which you yourself have come to trust. Be careful not to provide nourishment to the never-ending drama that stretches between parents and their children: it consumes a great deal of the energy of the young and it preys on the parents' love – which remains warm and alive even where it cannot comprehend. Do not seek their advice and do not count on their understanding; but you may be certain of a love like an inheritance in safekeeping for you; you can be sure that it contains a power and benediction that can stay with you, however far you may journey.

It is as well that very soon you will be embarking on a profession which will make you independent and will oblige you to look to yourself in every respect. You will have to wait patiently to see if your inner life finds itself too constrained by the nature of that profession. I believe that it is very hard and very demanding, carries a heavy burden of conventions, and leaves scarcely any room for an individual to interpret its requirements for himself. But your solitariness will be a quiet place, a homestead for you, however strange the circumstances that may surround you, and by its means you will always find your true path. All my good wishes are ready to accompany you, and I have faith in you.

Yours

Rainer Maria Rilke

V

Rome, 29 October 1903

My dear Sir,
It was in Florence that I received your letter of 29 August, and now, these two months later, I am replying to it. Do forgive me for the delay – it is because I prefer not to write letters while actually travelling, for I need more for them than just the obvious necessaries: a little quiet and privacy, and circumstances that are not too unfamiliar.

We got to Rome about six weeks ago and it was at a season when it was deserted, was sweltering, was Rome at its most infamously feverish, and this together with some practical difficulties caused us to be surrounded by a never-ending confusion, so that we felt burdened by the foreignness and by our homelessness. It should be added to this that Rome (for those who do not yet know it) in the first few days can seem mournful and oppressive: it is on account of the lifeless and drear museum-atmosphere it exhales, because of the lavish profusion of the antiquities (by means of which a little of the present gets its daily bread) unearthed and laboriously restored; because of the measureless over-veneration of all these displaced and ruined things, sponsored by academics and philologists and imitated by all the run-of-the-mill Italy-tourists – of things which in essence are no more than haphazard relics of a time that is not, and was never meant to be, our own. In the end, after weeks of daily resistance you are, although a little dazed, yourself again and you say to yourself: No, there is certainly no more beauty to be found here than there is anywhere else, and all these objects, admired from generation to generation, mended by many workmen's hands – no, they signify nothing, are nothing, have no heart and are of no true value: and yet there is great beauty here, for there is great beauty everywhere. Lively and never-ending, the waters pass over the great aqueducts and flow into the city, into the many piazzas, dancing over the bowls of white stone, spreading to fill the generous width of the basins, they murmur by day and murmur more loudly by night; and night is immense and is filled with stars and soft with breezes. And here are gardens and never-to-be-forgotten avenues and flights of steps, steps of Michelangelo's invention, steps made to resemble cascades of water descending, step after step, broad and declining, identical wave after wave. By means of such impressions one may collect oneself, win oneself back from the insistence of the talk and the chatter of the multitude (and *how* it chatters!); and gradually you come to recognise the very few things that have something everlasting, something that you can love, and something private in which you may share.

I am still lodging in the city, near the Capitol and not far from the finest equestrian sculpture that has survived for us from Roman times, that of Marcus Aurelius. But in a few weeks I shall be moving into a quiet, simple room – an old pavilion, lost in the depths of a great park and hidden from the city, its noise and its hazards. I shall live there all winter and will be glad of its great stillness, from which I have expectations of diligent and valuable *time*...

There, where I shall be more at home, I will write you a longer letter and in it I shall have something to say about your own writing. Just for now, I must tell you (and perhaps it was a mistake not to do so sooner) that the book of which you told me in your letter (and which you said had some of your work in it) has not reached me here. Was it perhaps sent back to you from Worpswede? (For one may not redirect packages to other countries.) That would be the most agreeable explanation and I trust you will confirm that it is so. I do hope that it did not get lost – although, sadly, losses are no rarity where the Italian post is involved.

I would have been pleased to receive the book (as I am with every message from you), and if there are poems you have written since (and if you trust me with them) I would always read, re-read and enter into them as fully and sincerely as I can. With my good wishes and my regards,

Yours

Rainer Maria Rilke

VI

Rome, 23 December 1903

My dear Herr Kappus,

You shall not be lacking a letter from me, with Christmas on the way and with yourself perhaps feeling the weight of your solitude more than usual amidst all the festivity. But if you do feel that it is great then be glad of it: for what (you might ask yourself) would a solitude be worth that lacked greatness? There is only *one* kind of loneliness, and it *is* great and is not easy to bear; and almost all of us have known hours which we would gladly have bartered against *any* kind of company, however cheap or banal, against the least semblance of any accommodation at all, even with something second-rate, something unworthy. And yet it may be at such times especially that loneliness is liable to grow, for its growing is as hard as a boy's growing-up and as bitter as the genesis of spring. You must not let that mislead you. What is required is this: solitariness, great inner solitariness. The going-into-oneself and the hours on end spent without encountering anyone else: it is this we must be able to achieve. To be as lonely as we were when we were children, with the grown-ups going to and fro around us, utterly tied-up in matters which seemed grave and grand to us, for they appeared so very business-like and we had not the least idea what they were doing.

And if one day we come to recognise that their occupations are paltry, their activities sterile and absolutely out of touch with life, then why not look upon them just as a child would look at something alien to it, gazing out at it from the depths of its own world, the acreage of its loneliness – which is itself a task, a position, an occupation. Why should one wish to exchange the child's wise incomprehension for rejection and contempt? Incomprehension amounts to solitariness of a kind, whereas by rejection and contempt we become part and parcel of the very things we had hoped they would save us from.

Think, my dear Sir, of the world you carry inside yourself, and give those thoughts whatever name you please, whether you call them the remembrance of your childhood, or the yearning to possess your future. But pay attention to what grows up within you and give it precedence over the things you are aware of all around you. What goes on deep within you is deserving of all your love: it is upon *that* you must work, at whatever cost, and not waste too much energy and too much time in trying to verify your attitude to other people. Who is to say that you even *have* any such attitude?

I know very well that your occupation is onerous and that it contradicts much that is in your nature, and I foresaw your protestations and knew they were bound to come. Now that you have uttered them I have no means to reassure you. I can only ask you to think if all professions are not like this, crammed with exigencies, filled with hostility towards the individual, and charged with the hatred of those others who have dumbly and resentfully settled into a routine of Lenten duty. The station in life you are now required to occupy is no more heavily laden with conventions, prejudices and absurdities than any other station in life; if there are some that offer the semblance of a greater freedom, there is nevertheless not one that is intrinsically open and accommodating and genuinely in touch with the great concerns that are life's real substance. Only the individual who stays solitary can be like a thing, a thing subject to the fundamental laws. And when someone walks out into the day as it begins to dawn or when he gazes out into the so richly eventful evening and is filled with a sense of what is happening then all his 'social standing' will fall away, as from a dead man, though he stands there in the very midst of life. Everything that you must now experience as an officer, my dear Herr Kappus, would have struck you in just the same way in any of the existing professions;

and even had you been without position and had, independently, sought free and individual social relationships, you would still not have been spared this feeling of constraint. – It is everywhere the same, and that is nevertheless no cause for fear or for sadness; if you find little in common between yourself and other people, then try to grow better acquainted with *things*, for they will not fail you; and there are still the nights, there is the wind blowing through the trees and over many lands; in the world of objects and of animals everything stays full of happenings – in which *you* may share; and children stay just as you were when you were a child, as sad and as joyful; and each time you think about your childhood you will again dwell among them, among those lonesome children, where grown-ups count for nothing and where their dignity is meaningless.

And if you should find it sad and painful to recall your childhood and all the simple, quiet, things that were bound up with it, because you can no longer believe in God who was everywhere present in it, then, dear Herr Kappus, you should ask yourself if you have, truly, lost God? Is it not rather that you had never possessed him? For – when do you suppose that loss occurred? And, moreover, can you really believe that a child could possess him? the One whom grown men can scarcely bear, whose weight crushes the old and wise? Can you believe that anyone who truly possessed him could lose him – as anyone might lose a pebble? Or do you not rather think that a man who had once possessed him could thenceforth only be lost *by* him? But, if you come to recognise that he was not present even then, neither in your childhood nor before it, when you begin to sense that Christ was led astray by his yearning, Mohammed betrayed by his pride – and when in dread you realise that he is *still* not present, not even at this moment that we speak of him – then what could make it right for you to search and pine and mourn, as for one dead, for one who never was?

Why can you not believe that he is the One-who-is-yet-to-come, the forever-awaited, the future One, the ultimate fruit of the tree of which we ourselves are the leaves? What stands in the way of your projecting his birth forward, into the times yet to come, and of living your own life as if it were some wonderful, some melancholy day within the history of a great gestation? For, do you not see how everything that takes place is ever and again a beginning, and might it not be *his* beginning, since beginning in itself is always of such beauty? Surely, if he himself is the most perfected, then there must have been lesser ones preceding him so that he might choose himself from a sufficiency, a more-than-abundance? Does he not *have* to be the last, if everything is to be comprehended in him? And what meaning would there be in us, if the one we crave had already been?

Just as the bees gather their honey, so we ourselves draw what is sweetest from all that there is and build him. We begin with lesser things, with what is unremarkable (so long as there is love in it), with work and the repose that comes after, with stillness or with one small, individual delight, with everything we accomplish on our own with no disciples, no accomplices: we begin to create him, whom we shall never know, just as our ancestors were never to experience ourselves. And nonetheless they, those long-gone people, are present in us, are present in our predispositions, in the weighting of our destinies, in the blood that sings in us and in gestures that rise out of the depths of time.

Is there anything that could take from you your hope that you may one day dwell in him – who is the most distant and the utmost?

My dear Herr Kappus: celebrate Christmas in the pious belief that it may be just your fear of life that he requires, still, for his beginning; these days of your transition are perhaps the very time for all that is within you to be at work on him, just as when you were still a child you used to work on him so breathlessly. You must stay patient and must keep good faith, and you should think that at the very least you should not make his coming any harder than Earth makes hard the advent of the spring.

I wish you happiness and good cheer.

Yours

Rainer Maria Rilke

VII

Rome, 14 May 1904

My dear Herr Kappus,

A long time has passed since your last letter reached me. Do not hold that against me: first it was work, then there were distractions, and lately it has been poor health that has time and again kept me from sending you the answer which (as I would have preferred it) should have been the fruit of quiet and profitable days. I am now feeling a little better again (the beginning of Spring with its cruel and fickle changes was hard, even here), and I take this opportunity, my dear Herr Kappus, to send you greetings and, as I am truly pleased to do, to comment here and there on your letter, as best I can.

Look: I have copied out your sonnet, because it struck me as simple and beautiful, born to the form in which it moves with such quiet good manners. It is the best of the poems of yours that I have been permitted to see. And now I am making you a present of the copy, for I know that it is important and can be a new experience to rediscover a work of one's own in another's handwriting. You must read the poem as if it were a stranger to you: you will feel at the deepest level how very much it is your own.

It has given me pleasure to read the sonnet and your letter often, and I thank you for both.

Do not let yourself be misled, in your solitariness, by the recognition that something in you would very much prefer to be rescued from it: it is just this feeling which, if you use it quietly and nobly and as if it were a tool, will help you to expand your solitude to cover a wide territory. Encouraged by the conventions, most people have found easy solutions to every problem

– the easiest aspects of whatever is easy; and yet it is clear that we were meant to stay with what is hard; all living creatures hold fast to it and everything in nature grows and protects itself in its own manner and stays an entity in its own terms – strives to stay one at whatever cost and against whatever opposition. There is little that we understand, but our conviction that we must stay in touch with what is difficult will not desert us: it is good to be solitary, for solitude is hard, and that something is hard must be just one more reason why we should do it.

Loving is good too, for love is hard. The fondness of one person for another – it may be that this is the most difficult task that we are set, the most extreme, the ultimate trial and proof, and the task for which all other tasks were no more than a preparation. And this is why young people, novices still in everything, are not yet *capable* of love; they have yet to learn it. They have, with their whole being, with all the strength they can summon to their anxious, lonely, upward-striving hearts, to learn how to love. And every apprenticeship is a lengthy and sequestered time, so that loving for a long time to come and far into any life means: loneliness, a heightened, deepened solitariness, for anyone who loves. Furthermore, loving is not something that can at once be called a flowering, a surrender, a union with another human being (for what sense is there in uniting what is still unclear, undistinguished, incomplete?): it is a high occasion for the individual spirit to ripen and to develop into something in itself, to become a world, to become a world in one's own self for someone else's sake: it is a great, immoderate demand upon the self, choosing and summoning it to far-distant places. It is in this sense only, as an imperative to work upon the self ('to hearken and to hammer, by night and by day'), that young people should be permitted to make use of the love that is granted them. The flowering, the surrender and the sharing are not yet for them (they will be obliged to scrimp and to save for a long time yet), for this is love's culmination, the thing for which entire human lifetimes are perhaps still scarcely sufficient.

It is in this that young people are so frequently and so

grievously mistaken; for they (who by nature utterly lack patience) hurl themselves at each other when love overcomes them and scatter themselves abroad in whatever state they may be – in all their prodigality, confusion, madness...But what can come of it? What is Life to make of such a pile of half-broken offerings...which they themselves designate their togetherness, and would be quite prepared to call their happiness, their destiny? Each is lost for the other's sake, and loses the other, and loses many more who were yet to come; loses the openness, the possibility, and barters the advent and departure of everything that is quiet and full of portent – against a barren ignorance that can lead on to nothing except aversion, disappointment and deprivation, and to a rescue by means of one of the numerous conventions set up, like so many public shelters, alongside this most dangerous of paths. No other area of human experience is as well-furnished with conventions as this is: here are life-belts of the most varied invention, boats and buoyancy-packs; our corporate ingenuity has known how to fashion safety-aids of all conceivable kinds, for since society has chosen to see love as a diversion it has also been obliged to provide it with an easy image – as safe and as harmless as any commonplace recreation.

To be sure, many young people who love wrongly, which is to say prodigally and not in private (and the average person will never grow far from this), feel oppressed by a sense of failure and long to make something viable and fruitful of their condition. Their very nature tells them that the problems of love cannot be solved publicly, by consensus of one kind or another, any more than all the other problems that truly matter; that these are matters, intimate matters, between one person and another, which in every case demand a new, a particular and *always* an individual solution: yet how can they, who have already hurled themselves together and let no boundaries or differences survive between them, and who in consequence no longer possess anything of their own, how can *they* find any way that might lead them out of themselves – out of the depths of the loneliness they have already spilled and scattered? All that they do is born of their common helplessness, and if in all good faith they should try to avoid whatever convention they have identified (most commonly, marriage) they rush instead into the welcoming embrace of some obvious but just as deadly formula; for there is nothing anywhere around them that is not a convention; whatever people do that comes of uninspired and over-hasty union will *always* be conventional; every relationship that results from such foolishness has its own conventions, however unusual (which means, in the commonplace view, immoral) it may be; and even separation would prove to be a conventional formula, a haphazard, anonymous decision, feeble and inconsequential.

Anyone who considers carefully will see that love is difficult, just as dying is difficult, and that no formula, no solution, no safe byways or passwords for it have been discovered; no unifying, abiding principles are to be found for these two tasks of ours which we keep shrouded and concealed; we carry them and we pass them on to others without revealing them. But in the same measure that we attempt to live our lives as *individuals*, these great concerns will move nearer to each of us. The demands that the heavy task of love makes on our development are larger than life and we, as novices, are not yet capable of meeting them. But if we can endure, can take up the weight of that love as our apprenticeship and as our burden – rather than lose ourselves among the numerous trivial and trivialising games by which people try to hide from the weightiest weight of their destiny – then perhaps those who will one distant day succeed us may notice some small advantage, some relief. And that would mean much.

For we are only now beginning to view the relations between one human being and another objectively and without prejudging them, and our attempts to live in such relations have no exemplars to assist them. Nonetheless there is something in the groundswell of our times that seeks to aid our first uncertain efforts.

It will not be forever that girls and women, in their new and individual flowering, will mimic the ways and wickednesses of men and follow their professions. After the precariousness of these transitions we shall be able to judge whether women have not undergone the profusion and the variousness of such (often ludicrous) disguises only in order to cleanse their own most individual nature from the distorting influences of the other sex. Women, in whom life dwells and tarries more directly, more fruitfully and more trustingly, will surely have grown into a riper and more human humanity than the more light-weight male – who bears the burden of no living fruit which might draw him deeper than life's surfaces, and who in his haste and presumption undervalues what he believes he loves. Born of sorrow and humiliation, this humanity of women will (just as soon as they have rid themselves of the conventions of mere womanliness by a revolution in their social standing) show itself quite plainly; and the men who even now *still* cannot sense that its day is approaching will be taken by surprise and defeated by it. One day (and there are already dependable signs which tell of this and which shed light upon it, especially in the northern countries), one day there will be girls and women who are no longer so called as a mere antithesis to the male, but as people in their own right, the words no longer suggesting a complement, a boundary – but life and being: the female human being. This advance (much against the liking, to begin with, of the men it leaves behind) will transform our love-experience which is still so full of misunderstandings: it will fundamentally reshape it, making of it a transaction between one *person* and another *person* – and no longer between 'man' and 'woman'. And this so-much-more-human love (which will enact itself with infinite considerateness and gentleness, binding and loosing with clarity and with kindness) will have taken for its model what we now labour and strive to bring about: the love by means of which two lonelinesses may protect, contain and acknowledge one another.

And one last thing: never believe that the generous love that was imposed on you when you were a boy was a lost experience. How can you be sure that there were not great and noble impulses ripening within you then, and precepts by which you still live, even today? I believe that that love remains so mighty, so powerful in your remembrance, because it was your first profound experience of being alone; and the first time that you worked upon your inner life. All my good wishes to you, my dear Herr Kappus.

Yours

Rainer Maria Rilke

VIII

Borgeby-gård, Flädie, Sweden, 12 August 1904

I would like to talk to you again a little, my dear Herr Kappus, even though I can say scarcely anything helpful. You have had many and grievous sorrows and they have passed away. And you tell me that their passing, too, has been hard for you and unsettling. But I beg you to consider: did not these sorrows go right through you – and not merely past you? Has there not been a great deal in you that has changed? Were you not somewhere, in some part of your nature, transformed while you were so sorrowful? The truly dangerous and malignant griefs are the griefs that we wear in public, trying to crowd them out: like sicknesses given incompetent or cursory treatment they only retreat, to break out again after a brief remission even more dreadfully; and they collect within us to become life itself, they are all life unlived, rejected, cast away; and we may die of them. If we could see a little further than our knowledge, could look over and above the ramparts of our intuition, we would perhaps bear our sorrows more trustingly than we do our happinesses. For it is at just *those* moments that something unfamiliar enters into us, something unknown; our senses, inhibited and shy, fall silent; everything within us shrinks back, there is silence, and at its centre this new thing, strange to us all, stands mutely there.

I believe that virtually all our griefs are moments of energy, and that we experience them as paralysis only because we have grown deaf to the life of our alienated feelings; because we are left on our own with this strange thing that has entered us; because everything we trust in and are accustomed to has, for a moment, been snatched away from us; because we stand in the midst of a transition and cannot stand still there. That is why even sorrow is transitory: the new thing that has supervened has entered into our heart, has occupied its innermost chamber and is no longer even there – it has already entered our blood. And we shall not discover what it was. We could easily be persuaded that nothing at all had passed, and yet we have been changed as a house changes when a guest enters it. We cannot say who has come, we shall perhaps never know. But there are many indications that it is the future that enters into us in this way, in order to be transformed within ourselves, long before it actually occurs. And that is why it is so essential to stay solitary and attentive when in the midst of sorrow: for the apparently uneventful, petrified instant at which our future takes possession of us stands so much closer to life than does that other noisy, random instant at which it happens to us, as it were, from outside. The quieter, the more patient, the more open we can be when we are sorrowful, the more steadily and profoundly this new thing will enter into us, the better we shall assimilate it, the more surely it will be *our own* destiny; and one day when it 'happens' (that means: when from ourselves it goes out to others), we shall feel that we are most intimately related and close to it. That is important. It is important (and by and by our evolution will tend towards this) for us to encounter nothing alien to us, only that which has for a long time been our own. We have already had to rethink so many theories of planetary motion; in the same way we shall, little by little, learn to recognise that what we call destiny proceeds *from* humankind, is not introduced to us from outside. It was only because so many had not absorbed their destinies while they were still within them that they were unable to recognise what was proceeding from them – it seemed so alien that in their confusion and alarm they concluded that it must just now have entered them, for they would swear they had never before discovered anything like this in themselves. Just as we have for so long been mistaken about the progression of the sun, we continue to misunderstand the progression of what is to come. The future stands fast, my dear Herr Kappus, while we ourselves move through infinite Space.

How could things *not* be difficult for us?

And speaking again of solitariness: it becomes ever clearer that this is not something that we can choose to have or to do without. We *are* solitary. We may deceive ourselves about this and we may make believe that it is otherwise. But that is all. How much better to admit our solitude, indeed to accept it as our absolute point of departure. But that of course is when we shall feel dizzy, for we shall have been all at once deprived of every mark on which our eyes were accustomed to rest; nothing that was near us remains, and what is far is infinitely far away. If someone were to be plucked from the safety of his own small room and, unprepared and almost instantaneously, set down upon the heights of some great mountain-range, he would surely experience something very like this: a never-to-be-equalled sense of insecurity, of having fallen into the power of something nameless, would virtually destroy him; he would feel as if he were falling, or had been hurled out into space, or had been shattered into a thousand fragments: what appalling fictions his brain would need to construct to account for what his senses feel and to seek to explain it! It is in exactly this way that all measure, all distance, is distorted when one is left in isolation: of such distortions many more are all at once born, and, just as for the man on the mountain-top, there will be strange chimaerae and never-before-experienced sensations which seem to grow and grow far beyond anything that anyone can bear. And yet it is important for us to experience this too. We must accept our destiny however far it may chance to take us: everything, including the inconceivable, must be acceptable within it. In the end this is the only valour that is asked of us: to be brave in the face of the most unheard-of, the most marvellous, the most inexplicable things that we may possibly encounter. That mankind has been pusillanimous in this respect has done endless harm to life itself: all the phenomena we call 'apparitions', all the so-called 'spirit-world', death, all these things so closely akin to us have been fended-off, day after day, and so thoroughly purged from our lives that the senses by which we might have grasped them have atrophied. To say nothing at all of God. But the fear of the unexplainable has not only impoverished the existence of the solitary spirit: relations between person and person are just as much constrained by it, similarly dragged from the stream of limitless possibility and cast upon a sterile shore upon which nothing moves. For it is not indolence alone that makes human relationships repeat themselves, time after time, with such unutterable monotony and staleness: it is a shrinking from any fresh and unforeseeable experience which we fear will be too much for us. And yet, only one who is prepared for everything, one who will exclude nothing, can dwell in a *living* relationship with another and can fully live out even his own destiny. For if we can imagine each individual destiny as a greater or lesser space, we shall see that few people come to know more than a corner of their room – a window-seat, a strip of carpet to pace up and down. And this gives them security of a kind. And yet, a perilous uncertainty is so very much more human – just as in Poe's stories the prisoners feel constrained to grope out the dimensions of their terrifying dungeon, to familiarise themselves with the unspeakable horror in which they dwell. We, on the other hand, are not imprisoned. There are no snares, no man-traps, set about us, and there is really nothing that need frighten or torment us. We are set down in life as in the element with which we are most in accord, and we have furthermore come, through millennia of adaptation, so to *resemble* life that (if we remain motionless) we successfully mimic everything around us and can scarcely be distinguished from it. We have no grounds for suspicion of our world, for it is not hostile to us. If there are terrors then they are our terrors, if chasms, then those chasms too are ours; if there are dangers then it is for us to learn to love them. And if we arrange our lives in accordance with the precept that teaches us always to hold to what is difficult – then everything that still appears most alien will become all that is best-trusted, most dependable. How can we ever forget those ancient myths which stand close to the origins of every race of people? the legends of dragons which, at the very last instant, transform themselves into princesses: it may be that all the dragons in our lives are princesses and that they only wait to see us, for once at least, handsome and valiant. Perhaps every thing of terror in our lives is in its deepest nature a helpless thing that craves our help.

So you must not be appalled, dear Herr Kappus, if sorrow should loom up before you greater than any you have ever known, if an agitation like that of light through drifting clouds casts shadow on your hands and on all that they perform. For you will know that something is at work on you, that life has not forgotten you and that it holds you in its hand. It will not let you fall. Why should you want to exclude from your life any grief, any anxiety, any heavy-heartedness? For you cannot know how such circumstances might be at work upon you. Why should you persecute yourself with questions as to where all this originates, what it might lead to? For you know very well that you are in transition, and that you wished above all else to be transformed. If something in your life seems sickly, then you should consider that sickness is the means by which an organism rids itself of something alien to it, you should help it to be ill, to experience all its sickness, to let it break out, for that is how it will get better. There is so much, dear Herr Kappus, going on in you just now; you will need to be as stoical as an invalid and as hopeful as a convalescent, for you are perhaps both and even more, for you are also the doctor in charge of his own treatment. In all maladies there are nevertheless times at which a doctor can do no more than wait. Insofar as you are your own doctor this, above all, is what you should now be doing.

Do not watch yourself too closely. And do not be over-hasty in drawing conclusions from your experience; simply let it happen to you. For else you may too readily look back reproachfully (and that means – moralistically) at your own past, which has of course its share in everything that happens to you now. What still affects you from among the blunderings, the hopes, the longings of your boyhood is not at all what you now remember and make judgements on. The special circumstances of a helpless, solitary childhood are so hard, so complex, and are at the mercy of so many influences (and at the same time so unrelated to any real context of living), that if what seems like vice appears in it we must not be too quick to label it as vice. We should in general be very circumspect with names: it is so often on the *name* of a transgression that a life is shipwrecked, and not on the individual, nameless, act-in-itself, which may have been of an absolute necessity to that life – and might perhaps have been effortlessly assimilated by it. And the energy required seems so much to you only because you over-value 'success'; that is not the 'greatness' to which you lay claim, although you are right in your general feeling; the greatness is that there was something already present which you were permitted to set in place of that deception, something real and true. Without it, your 'success' would have been no more than a moral reflex of no broader significance, and not the sample of your life that it has now become. Of your life, dear Herr Kappus, on which I reflect with so many good wishes. Do you recollect how, from childhood on, that life of yours reached out in longing for the 'grown-ups'? I see it now turning from the 'grown' and craving for the 'greater'. That is why it does not cease to be hard but it is also why it will not cease to grow.

If I have one more thing to tell you it is this: do not believe that he who seeks to console you dwells effortlessly among the quiet and simple words which sometimes content you. His own life holds much trouble and sorrow, and it falls far short of them. But if it were not so he could not have found those words.

Yours

Rainer Maria Rilke

IX

Fruborg. Jonsered, Sweden, 4 November 1904

My dear Herr Kappus,
During this time that has gone by without a letter, I have been travelling sometimes and at other times so busy that I could not write. Even today I am finding it hard to write for I have had to write many letters already and my hand is weary. If only I could *dictate* I would have much to say to you, but as things are you must make do with only a few words in answer to your own long letter.

I think of you often, my dear Herr Kappus, and with such a concentration of good wishes that it really should be of some help to you. Whether my *letters* are truly of any assistance to you – that is something I sometimes wonder. You must not answer: Yes, of course they are. Instead, receive them quietly and with not too many thanks, and let us, please, wait and see what may come of them.

It may not be helpful at this time for me to discuss particular concerns of yours; for all that I could say to you about your predisposition to doubt, about your inability to harmonise your inner to your outer life, or about all the other things that distress you, is still just what I have said to you before: that I hope that you will find in yourself the patience to be able to endure and the simplicity to be able to believe; that you may more and more come to have faith in whatever is hard and in your solitariness even among other people. And for the rest – you must let life have its way with you. Life is right in any event, believe me.

As regards your emotions: every emotion that concentrates and exalts you is pure. What is impure is an emotion that takes hold of only one side of your nature, and will in consequence distort it. Any thought that can stand face-to-face with your childhood is, surely, good. Whatever makes more of you than you have ever been before, even at your best times, is all that it should be. Every heightened moment is good if it suffuses all your blood, if it is not dark or drunken, if it is transparent and unclouded even in its depths. Do you understand what I am saying?

And as regards your doubting, it may yet grow to be a useful attribute if you can school it properly. It must grow knowledgeable, must learn to be critical. You should, whenever it tries to spoil something for you, ask it *why* such-and-such a thing is ugly, you should insist on being shown its evidence, you must cross-examine it: perhaps you will leave it defeated and discouraged – or perhaps it may make a fight of it. You must nevertheless not give in, you must make your case and, watchful and consistent, you must do so each and every time; the day will come when out of one who used to be a vandal you will have made one of your best men – perhaps the most knowledgeable of the artisans at work upon the building of your life.

That is all, dear Herr Kappus, that I can say to you for today. But I am posting you an offprint of a little poem that has just appeared in the Prague journal *Deutsche Arbeit* and in which I can continue to speak to you of life and death, and of the splendour and the greatness of both.

Yours

Rainer Maria Rilke

X

Paris, 26 December 1908

I want you to know, my dear Herr Kappus, how glad I was to receive that fine letter from you. The news you give me, real and communicable as it now sounds again, seemed good to me, and the longer I considered it the more genuinely good it seemed. I had really meant to write you this for Christmas Eve, but what with my work, in which, this winter, I live in all kinds of ways and with no interruption, the festival arrived so swiftly that I scarcely had time to make the most necessary purchases, let alone to write letters.

Nevertheless I thought of you often during the holidays, and I imagined how quiet you must be in your lonely fortress among the empty hills – with the great south winds racing across them as if they wanted to gulp them down in great pieces.

There must be an enormous silence to give space for so much sound, so much movement, and when one remembers that in addition to all this, accompanying it, there is the distant presence of the sea, perhaps the very innermost sound in this whole prehistoric harmony, then one can only hope that you will permit this marvellous isolation to work upon you, for it is something that can never be deleted from your life; it will abide with you as an anonymous voice and will direct you in all your living and doing – in the same way, perhaps, that the blood of progenitors moves in us unceasingly, mingling with our own to make of us the unique, the unrepeatable being we are and will remain through all the changes in our lives.

Yes, I am happy that you have this firm and expressible way of life available to you: the rank; the uniform; the duty: all these tangible and circumscribed things which (in such surroundings and with so limited and isolated a company of men) take on seriousness and necessity far above the merely theatrical and time-filling aspects of the military profession, call for a vigilant application, and not only make room for but actually *teach* independence and circumspection. All we really need is to find ourselves in circumstances that work on us and, from time to time, confront us with things that are great and natural. Even art is just one way of living, and we may be preparing ourselves for it without even knowing that we do so, however we may be living. We are closer to it, on more neighbourly terms, in everything that is real than in the various half-artistic professions – which in fact, by the pretence that they are nearly-art, injure and defame all true art; as does all journalism, almost all criticism, and three-quarters of what is called literature or would wish to be called literature. I am glad that you have withstood the dangers of straying into all that, and that instead you stay lonely and valiant in some place that is rough and real. I hope that the year to come will sustain and strengthen you in it.

Ever yours,

Rainer Maria Rilke

Rainer Maria Rilke, Franz Xaver Kappus

The letters from the famous poet Rainer Maria Rilke to the younger officer cadet (and aspiring poet) Franz Xaver Kappus, preceded by Kappus's own introduction, tell a great deal of their own story. However some readers will wish to learn more of the background to this text. I have thought it better that this material should follow the letters so as not to pre-empt the element of story-telling that they already contain.

René Maria Rilke was born in 1875 in Prague, to middle-class parents. After an over-protected and emasculating infancy and childhood he was sent to military schools, first at St Pölten and later at Mährisch-Weisskirchen. There he was, not surprisingly, utterly wretched. In the end and at his own request he was sent home on the grounds of ill-health. (Josef Rilke, his father, after ten years of better than adequate service as a cadet in the artillery, had failed to gain his commission and had in the end also been discharged on the grounds of his poor health.)

As a fifteen-year-old youth Rilke believed for a while that it was still his destiny to be a soldier. Instead he grew into a gifted student-dandy who fell frequently and easily in love and out again. Gradually it became clear that his goal was to become a writer.

Throughout his young manhood Rilke developed as a precociously fluent poet and man of letters. Later, his travels were to take him to Russia, to Spain, to Paris and to a host of other places in Europe, to North Africa and Egypt. He became the lover of the astonishing Lou Andreas-Salomé (who persuaded him to change his *René* to *Rainer*), and he became the protégé and friend of an army of famous, gifted or aristocratic Europeans. He was all his life an enthusiastic, careful writer of letters, of which he kept hand-written copies. The letters to

Kappus are perhaps the most outstanding among the many important collections of Rilke letters (see pp. 127–8) but between June and November 1907 he wrote his wife, the sculptor Clara Westhoff, another important sequence of letters. From these she later made the selection published in 1952, long after Rilke's death, under the title *Briefe über Cézanne*.

During the years of his exchange of letters with Kappus, Rilke was practically all the time fruitfully engaged in his own writing. I have included, in the Chronology at the end of this text, the titles of his most important works of 1903 to 1908.

Franz Kappus, born in 1883, was only eight years younger than Rilke. His birthplace is given as Temesvar, a town in the southwest of Rumania near the Yugoslav border.

Kappus graduated from his military academy in 1903, and in 1908 and 1909 he served in South Dalmatia. (The 'distant presence of the sea' in Letter X refers to the Adriatic.) Later, Kappus was promoted to captain and posted to the War Ministry in Vienna. From 1914 to 1918 he was employed as a war correspondent. From 1919 to 1924 he worked as a journalist in Temesvar and Brno, and from 1925 he lived in Berlin. In 1945 he took part in establishing the postwar Liberal Democratic Party.

Twenty-nine titles are given as his literary legacy. They include comedies, satires, novels and novellas; nevertheless he is dismissed as a *Konversations-schriftsteller* – a writer of lightweight pieces – by one Rilke biographer, and this appears to be the generally held view. It also seems that, as he himself wrote, his life led him into the very circumstances from which Rilke's 'warm and kind concern' would have wished to protect him. It is interesting to note that by some date in 1903, and while the exchange of letters with Rilke was still alive, Kappus had passed out from the military academy and was already serving as a lieutenant in Vienna.

Chronology 1903–1909

1903 Paris – Rilke worked on *Rodin* Part I, published during this year. The third and last part of *Das Stundenbuch*, *Von der Armut und vom Tode*, was completed within a few days in Viareggio where Rilke had gone to recover – from Paris and from an unspecified illness.

1904 Rilke began to work on *Malte Laurids Brigge*. (This work, Rilke's strongly autobiographical experimental novel, did not appear in print until 1910.) Travels in Denmark and Sweden at the invitation of Ellen Key.

1905 Publication of *Das Studenbuch*. On 15 September Rilke left his lodgings in rue Cassette to visit Rodin at the latter's home, the Villa des Brillants in Meudon-Val-Fleury. He was invited to stay at Meudon and to act as Rodin's secretary.

1906 Work on *Neue Gedichte*. Death of Josef Rilke, his father. At Meudon, Rilke met George Bernard Shaw, who had come to sit for a Rodin portrait. Rilke was delighted with Shaw. Rodin, possibly angered by his disciple's enthusiasm for another master, quarrelled with Rilke and dismissed him on 10 or 11 May. Rilke, deeply hurt, returned to the rue Cassette. Rilke's visit to Belgium. First publication of *Die Weise von Liebe und Tod des Cornets Christoph Rilke*. (The *Cornet* was written in 1899 but was greatly revised in 1904 and again in 1906.) Much of the *Neue Gedichte* Part I was completed, and *Das Buch der Bilder* which first appeared in 1902 was published in a new and greatly expanded edition. In November, to Naples and Capri.

1907 In Capri until end of May when Rilke travelled to Rome

and thence returned to Paris. By 7 June he was again at rue Cassette. Lecture tour to Prague, Breslau, Vienna, followed by ten days in Venice. Then to Oberneuland to join his wife Clara and Ruth, their daughter. *Rodin* Part II completed on the basis of the recent Rodin lectures. At the end of the year, publication of *Neue Gedichte* Part I.

1908 By stages to Berlin. 29 February, return to Capri. 15 April, to Paris. Much of the *Neue Gedichte* Part II was written during this summer and the book published in December. On 31 August Rilke took over Clara's studio at the Hôtel Biron and later he moved to other accommodation in the same building. This remained his Paris home until 1911.

1909 At a meeting between Rilke and Rodin at the Hôtel Biron on 2 September, the rift between the two men was finally repaired. Perhaps as a result of this meeting, the sculptor moved into four rooms on the main floor of the Hôtel Biron in October. The building was eventually to become the Musée Rodin.